W9-DIR-682

UTILIZING TEACHER AIDES
IN
DIFFERENTIATED STAFFING

UTILIZING TEACHER AIDES IN DIFFERENTIATED STAFFING

HOWARD BRIGHTON

**PENDELL
PUBLISHING
COMPANY**

International Standard Book Number: 0-87812-016-5
Library of Congress Catalog Card Number: 75-168584

To Eva, Ruby, Wally and in Memory to Howard.

CONTENTS

CONTENTS (Cont'd)

CONTENTS (Cont'd)

CONTENTS (Cont'd)

INTRODUCTION

Today's administrator may find himself faced with the task of easing the professional teachers into managerial roles. The increased use of teacher aides is placing new managerial responsibilities on professional teachers who may or may not like this change; and who may or may not have the skills required to cope with the resulting situations.

The concept of the instructional team has been defined as the extension of master teachers to supervisory direction of non-professional assistants in the classroom. Under this concept, the teacher becomes the team leader who has the responsibility of coordinating available educational resources to facilitate the educational growth of the whole child.

Ideally, the professional teacher is trained and certified to analyze the instructional needs of pupils and to initiate educational activities to meet these needs. Since the professional teacher should determine student needs and activities, they then must inform the aide of the objectives and the ideas behind them.

In selecting duties for their nonprofessional aides, the teachers must use their best professional judgment in selecting tasks which will enable the aides to feel that they are making valuable contributions to the educational processes in the classroom. These tasks must allow the aides to make a worthwhile contribution, but they must not allow the aides, either consciously or unconsciously, to infringe upon the authority of the professional teachers.

The aides must be informed of the objectives behind the activities they are assigned so that they will understand that their work is an integral part of the educational process. However, they must not be allowed the prerogative of expecting the professional teachers to explain and defend their decisions and actions. Such prerogative would place the aides on the same authority-level as their professional supervisor.

The teachers, without managerial experience, may be terrified at the idea of having an aide in their classroom. But most teachers, given the cooperation of the administration, the program coordinator and the aides, can develop managerial skill.

There is, of course the danger that supervising teachers who have poor self-concepts and doubts about their ability in the classroom, may view the aides as threats to their professional authority, may feel the necessity to constantly explain and defend themselves before the aides.

Where this kind of teacher-teacher aide relationship exists, students may find it difficult to determine who really is in charge. This may further detract from the teacher's self-concept and actually hamper their ability to control.

Such teachers, effective in the classrooms without the aides, might lose competence in the classroom situation in the presence of their supposedly supporting assistant.

Initially, teachers should be made aware that they will not be forced to accept the services of aides in the classrooms, but that they may have the services of aides either inside or outside of the classrooms but that they may have the services of aides either inside or outside of the classrooms on request. It should also be pointed out that because of varying classroom size and make-up, not all teachers need the assistance of an aide. This may help to reduce the danger of discord between the reluctant teachers and others who have or desire the services of aides.

Generally, permitting the teachers to take an active part in the aide selection process helps to assure that they will feel that they are the supervisors, and the aides, their assistants. It will also prevent many potential personality conflicts. When the teachers and the aides choose each other, they begin on a mutually attractive ground. To vindicate their choice, each works harder to make the relationship a success.

After a trial period, either the teachers or the aides should be permitted to suggest transfers. If the transfer of the aide is from one school to another or from one district to another, there will be less chance of reflection on either the teacher or the aide.

In the instance where a teacher rejects the idea of a classroom aide, interjection of a floating aide should be considered. The floating aide—one who is not assigned to a particular classroom but "floats" from class to class and school to school as needed—offers excellent means of developing the teacher's skills and self-confidence. Relatively short exposures to the teacher-aide relationship may tend to be developmental and less frightening than a permanent arrangement.

Our society today requires, and in the future will demand, significant educational changes which prescribe the use of master teachers and auxiliary teacher aides in the classroom.

The educational forecast indicates a continued and rapidly increasing need for planned efficient use of the professional educator's time. As the environment becomes more demanding, "hit or miss" employment of auxiliary teaching help can no longer be permitted.

Professional teacher organizations are becoming increasingly insistent in their demands for smaller classes, reduction of routine duties, and more time for individual pupil-teacher consultation, preparation, professional growth and other major responsibilities. These demands underscore the social need for incorporation of teacher aides in the classroom structure.

Paid teachers' aides were first employed extensively as an emergency means of meeting a serious war-time shortage of teachers in the 1940's. These aides were employed with very little preplanning of responsibilities, requirements and accountability. Lack of structure in the emergency program brought about confusion which caused professional teachers to view the idea of aides with distrust and often with open hostility.

The 1960's, ushering in a new era of education, projected a more realistic teacher aide program designed to meet the changing needs of schools and the challenge of the modern classroom.

Today's teacher aide program, facilitating a lively curriculum and a stimulating learning atmosphere for all students, offers a new and better approach to education.

It recognizes that in the course of a child's education he will have many needs which the professional teacher cannot find time to fill. It recognizes, too, that the education of the whole child projects, if not prescribes, many tasks for which the professional teacher has inadequate time.

By providing adult assistance in the classroom, it helps to ease the minor frustrations of students and to reduce the number of chores which harry the professional teacher.

Federal, state, and local governments charged with providing educational services are becoming increasingly aware that employment of aides will help school systems to attract and hold dedicated and creative master teachers. And with that in mind, they are becoming increasingly active in supporting the aide program.

Many community colleges are developing teacher aide training programs.

The teacher aide program, in order to be a meaningful vital part of the educational system, must have order and structure. Purpose, responsibility and function must be spelled out to provide a basis for understanding and cooperation. The program must have a definite structure which establishes authority and provides channels of communication. A program which does not have this structure takes on aspects of a stop-gap operation, subject to whims, special interests and prejudices.

Teacher aides in any school system will fall into several categories, some of which are educational, some clerical and some service.

Requirements for each aide category should be set by the State Department of Education, which should also define a certification and sanctioning system to ascertain that the requirements are met.

The State Department of Education should also retain responsibility for certification of the advanced teacher aides— those who will take on actual teaching duties—upon recommendation of their training institution. Other aide categories could be sanctioned locally, according to requirements set by the Department.

(Sanctioning implies giving credence to a practice after certain criteria have been met. Certification implies giving license to sanctioned practices, upon completion of defined requirements, by the state's top legally constituted educational authority.)

The superintendent (or other head of the local educational system) should be responsible for the employment and deployment of all aides within his system. But he may delegate authority for implementation and operation of the aide program to sub-administrators and/or to the local educational association should always be given a strong consultative role, if not an administrative one, in the program. It should also serve as the policing agency to see that the aides do not become "cheap" teachers.

While the community colleges are fast becoming the chief teacher aide training authority, the administrator should be responsible for the inservice training of aides within his system.

There are indications that efficient operation of the teacher aide program calls for at least eight teacher aide classifications. Each would be responsible for specific functions within the educational framework. Most schools could use one or more categories; few could use as many as eight.

Eight proposed aide categories follow:

1. Student Aides: elementary or secondary students who, either in a paid or voluntary capacity, help teachers in or outside the classroom.

2. Mother Aides: mothers of students who volunteer to assist the teacher with a variety of classroom connected activities other than teaching.

3. Father Aides: fathers of students who volunteer to assist the teacher with various classroom connected activities other than teaching and who, incidentally, serve as male-patterning figures in helping fatherless students in developing role identity.

4. Volunteer Aides: individuals, many of whom have unique talents and abilities, who volunteer their services in the classroom, and may float from classroom to classroom and from school to school (this is an open-ended category).

5. Special Aides: individuals with one special talent or proficiency whose services are usually available to more than one teacher. These are either volunteer or paid.

6. Practical Aides: those who perform clerical or service tasks for pay.

7. Certified Aides: those who, after a year of formal post high school training, are semi-qualified and can perform semi-instructional classroom activities under the supervision of a certified teacher. Paid.

8. Reader-Grader Aides: college graduates, who after screening to ascertain their capability, check compositions for errors in capitalization, punctuation, spelling, sentence structure, word usage and basic theme organization.

Paid aides, as a general rule, work out better than volunteers. The paid person seems to feel a greater obligation to perform designated functions at designated times. This makes it easier to coordinate his efforts with those of others. Such coordination yields the cooperative organized structure which operates with maximum proficiency and a minimum of confusion.

CHAPTER I

THE TEACHER AIDE CONCEPT

Our society promises to change in the future, perhaps even more rapidly and fundamentally than it has in the recent past. The gap between an attainable ideal and the actual situation, then, is likely to widen with each passing day unless the schools find ways to adjust to or direct some of the forces that are creating change.

Robert H. Anderson, *Teaching in a World of Change*, New York, Harcourt, Brace & World, 1966, p. 7.

The Teacher Aide Concept

Status of Contemporary Teacher Aide Programs

The task of writing a single brief job description for a teacher aide can prove to be a monumental task. Obtaining a job description of a contemporary teacher aide is like asking a blind man to describe water and enumerate its uses.

Present teacher aide programs range from the well-structured to the completely unstructured; from voluntary aides to paid aides; from the young to the old; from a few hours a month to 40 hours per week; from supervisory to menial tasks; from the well-educated to the illiterate; from the rich to the poverty stricken; and from police officers to petty thieves. The value of a teacher aide program consists of a myriad of challenging and hopeful advantages to modern education. The planned and proper use of auxiliary personnel could alleviate or eliminate many present educational problems.

11

Being pedantic, one could aptly describe the contemporary teacher aide concept as being in a state of complete "paraprosexia." (The fixation of attention upon an idea without structure or progress in developing the concept.) Empirical observation on the implementation of teacher aides into the educational system in a structural fashion overwhelmingly qualifies and validates this innovative service for the contemporary educational "ZEITGEIST" award.

What is the Teacher-Teacher Aide Team Concept?

The concept of an instructional team has been defined as the extension of master teachers to supervisory direction of nonprofessional assistants in the classroom. The teacher is the team leader and has the responsibility of coordinating the educational growth of the whole child.

When working with aides the teacher must rely on her professional judgment when assigning duties to her nonprofessional helper to enable the aide to feel that she is making a valuable contribution to the educative process. The aide must be flexible enough to do whatever the teacher requests. However, the teacher should realize the bounds of her professional duties and reserve those duties for her performance.

The teacher should assign tasks to the aide which will enable the aide to make a worthwhile contribution yet not usurp the professional power of the teacher. The introduction of an aide to a classroom will not reduce the teacher's actual teaching work load but will give her more time to perform her professional functions.

The professional teacher is trained and certified to perform certain functions in the education of children such as the analyzation of the instructional needs of the pupils and initiation of educational activities to meet these needs. It is the professional teacher who performs these tasks and, since it is the professional who determines the needs and activities, it is she who must inform the aide of the activities and the ideas behind them.

The aide must be informed of the ideas behind the activities so that she will feel she is an integral part of the educative process. By her attitude and inclusion or exclusion of the aide in planning activities, it is the teacher who makes or breaks the role of the teacher aide.

The key to a successful teacher-teacher aide relationship is free communication, flexibility of tasks and trust. The attitude of an effective team approach is:

"Which of us can learn how to perform this particular task in a way that will give the most help to the greatest number of pupils?"

How do Educational "Purists" View the Use of Teacher Aides?

Educational purists view the teacher aide concept with contempt. They look upon aides as flagrant violators of sound educational principles.

They view aides as unscrupulous invaders whose sole purpose is to exploit, plagiarize and contaminate the sound, time-tested values of education. They also believe that aides will usurp power and undermine the authority role of teachers, which will lead to an anarchical structure and insipid classroom leadership.

Purists feel the use of teacher aides is, with impunity, a gross violation of the traditional role reserved for the classroom teacher.

Even though the teacher aides are assigned and clearly understand that their role is secondary and limited, purists still believe the aides are a constant, potential threat. Purists say the teacher is placed in the position of either consciously or unconsciously vying with another adult, who may unwittingly and without conscious effort serve as a competitive adult force in the classroom. Students also are forced to choose between teacher and aide power positions on many individual matters.

Students are in a position to either consciously or unconsciously create events and situations that pit one adult power-figure against the other.

Once a teacher feels her position of authority is threatened, a great deal of her teaching time will be spent in rationalization and defensive activities. A basic defensive action is explanation and justification of classroom activities to her assigned aide.

Purists feel that, since few teachers are conditioned and trained in the use and management of teacher aides, their knowledge will limit and restrict teacher-student contact, because the teacher will have compulsory and perfunctory obligations which will remove her from student contact.

Past and Present Use of the Teacher Aide Concept

Teacher aides are not a new educational innovation; the use of aides is at least as old as planned education. Teacher aides, as used in the past and as presently used, will not meet future needs. In general, educators agree that our present educational system is in need of a structured aide program. They further agree that our society now requires and in the future will demand significant educational changes involving teacher aides.

The educational forecast points out a continued and rapidly growing need for a more efficiently planned use of the teacher's time. The throes of the present educational policy-making no longer provide for an environment in which a "hit or miss" auxiliary teaching help policy is satisfactory.

Speaking for their membership, professional teaching organizations have become more vociferous in their demands for reduction of routine matters, smaller class sizes, more time for individual pupil-teacher consultations, time for professional growth, preparation, and a host of lesser demands.

Paid teacher aides were first used extensively in the early 1940's. At this point in history, there was a serious teacher shortage along with a poor pay policy in our public schools, both due mainly to the depression of the 1930's. A third factor promoting use of paraprofessionals was the need for and cost of professionals to train personnel to meet the needs of accelerating war industries.

Aides were employed with a minimum of planning as an emergency. Teachers met this war-time emergency aid with disgust and open hostility.

One of the next major attempts to employ teacher aides was the Bay City, Michigan project in 1952. The project was sponsored by the Bay City Schools and Central Michigan University and was made possible by a Ford Foundation grant.

The Bay City program was predicated on a continued teacher shortage. The aide was an inducement for teachers to face the larger student-teacher ratios. The 1960's brought in a new era and a new, realistic aide program to meet the challenge of the classroom and changing needs of today's schools.

Present educational problems, spawned to greater awareness through professional negotiations, point to a need for better management of personnel to aid in the practical adjustment of professional time to student needs.

It is the primary responsibility of the teacher to provide his students with the best possible education. To fulfill this responsibility, he must actively search for a stimulating learning atmosphere, a lively curriculum for all students and new approaches to instruction.

Various professional organizations espouse the above demands, seeking relief from time-consuming, nonproductive, routine duties through recognized and approved practices that are conducive to the educational movement in all respects. This, in substance, means having the relief come from a legally certified, organizationally approved, and locally adopted semi-professional source.

Why the Nonprofessional?

Because a teacher is a human being, she cannot know everything there is to know, do everything there is to do nor play all the roles she should play in a single school day. During the course of a child's education he will have many needs which the teacher is incapable of fulfilling, yet he should have contact with persons who can and will satisfy his needs.

Many of the daily frustrations of the school child seem trivial to his adult teacher whose aim is to teach. But to the child, new to the social world of school, even minor frustrations can be grossly exaggerated and misinterpreted. There is a need for an adult to smooth the way, an adult who is mediator between student and professional and the new world of expectations. The professional needs this mediator, too, to assume some of the trivial nonprofessional chores which are a part of the organizational day in school.

In the contemporary school systems many functions which were primarily the responsibility of the professional teacher are being delegated to nonprofessionals because educators have learned that every moment a teacher spends on the noninstructional phases of her professional job is time she does not have to spend on her professional instructional function.

In contemporary education a new leadership role is being developed for professional teachers that will help lessen the noninstructional work load. As the teacher assumes the managerial position and learns to coordinate the talents and manpower available from teacher aides, she will become the pivotal person, responsible and accountable for insuring that education occurs in the classroom.[1]

What is Expected of Today's Teacher?

Today's teachers are expected to be all things, to all people, at all times, for all reasons, on all occasions that appear to be even remotely related to the school. The most frequent complaint registered by teachers is that of constantly being overloaded with non-academic or noninstructional duties in and out of the classroom.

According to a report by the Ford Foundation, classroom activities not requiring professional competence absorb from 21 to 69 per cent of the teacher's day.[2] Educators agree that no teacher, however competent she may be, can be effective unless she has time to teach. Good teachers require and demand time—time for preparation, delivery, evaluation, guidance, counseling, and observation.

As a result of the non-academic duties, innovative, dynamic and competent teachers find themselves trapped in the performance of ever-increasing time-consuming menial tasks. This practice results in outstanding teachers and prominent college students seeking careers other than teaching.

Contemporary teachers are faced with the required performance of many unrealistic but expected duties which could be performed by teacher aides.

---

[1] Garda W. Bowman and Gordon J. Klopf, "New Careers and Roles in the American School." A study conducted for the Office of Economic Opportunity, New York: Bank Street College of Education, September, 1967, p. 36-37, p. 153-154.

[2] Ford Foundation: Fund for the Advancement of Education, A Report for 1952-54, page 28, New York, Ford Foundation 1954.

17

Teacher aides could in most cases perform clerical and technical tasks not only better than teachers but with greater enthusiasm. In turn, teachers would be able to enhance their own self-image by doing tasks that they were professionally prepared to perform.

Listed are some of the more common duties expected of teachers; it is not minimal nor replete. No teacher would be expected or required to perform all of these duties, nor any of them to the same degree.

Bookkeeping and Storekeeping Duties:

1. Keep attendance records.

2. Keep academic records.

3. Collect money for educational materials.

4. Collect money for various fund drives.

5. Sell tickets to school activities.

6. Collect money for milk, hot lunch, or other types of school and classroom sales.

7. Order, return and operate audio-visual equipment.

School Related Obligations:

1. Supervise home room, study hall, lunchroom, detention room, halls, etc.

2. Supervise noon hour, recess and other activity periods.

3. Chaperone various school functions.

4. Drive the school bus.

Teaching Obligations:

1. Present and explain educational concepts to the students.

2. Plan and work with individual students.

3. Give guidance and counsel students on academic, vocational and personal concerns.

4. Develop audio-visual materials such as outlines, work-sheets, study guides, reading lists, projector overlays, display examples, etc.

5. Prepare and produce tests and study materials for students.

6. Read, evaluate and make suggestions on student work.

7. Serve as advisor on various class projects both in and out of school.

8. Supervise student teachers.

9. Confer with students and parents on pupil progress.

10. Maintain an active interest in school-community activities.

11. Plan joint projects, activities, or innovative ideas with fellow teachers.

12. Serve as an analytical observer.

13. Make written and oral reports to remedial sources.

14. Serve as a sensitive and understanding confidant.

Professional Obligations:

1. Keep abreast of current research and developments in the areas of the disciplines.

2. Attend school in-service training functions.

3. Continue professional education to avoid obsolescence of knowledge.

4. Read professional journals in order to keep up with new innovations and changes in teaching.

5. Participate in professional organizations.

6. Carry out experiments and research and report the findings.

All of these are realistic duties which need to be performed by someone in the educational system. The ultimate questions are: "Do all of these duties need to have the personal attention of a professional teacher?" and "Will the structural use of auxiliary personnel allow teachers more time to teach while at the same time bringing about an environment more conducive to learning?"

Why the Sudden Need for Teacher Aides?

Social, educational and economic factors have contributed to a sharp increase in the number of auxiliary personnel employed in schools and have evoked widespread interest in the teacher aide concept. [3]

Prior to World War II, few paid teacher aides were employed. However, many of the certified teachers of that era would barely qualify as a certified aide today. During World War II teacher aides were employed and the teachers were often openly

---

[3] *Auxiliary School Personnel: Their roles, Training and Institutionalization*, based on a nationwide study conducted for the U.S. Office of Economic Opportunity, Bank Street College of Education, New York, October, 1966.

hostile and negative toward the aides. Teachers viewed the aides with suspicion, distrust, and as active usurpers of professionalism. The non-teaching roles in schools, until the last two decades, were few, consisting primarily of the school custodian, lunchroom personnel, truant officers, minimal office help and, if fortunate, a part-time nurse.

Reorganization of the structural patterns in schools, expanded curriculum, differentiated roles for teachers, cooperative and team teaching, group work, seminar work, and individualized instruction have made teaching a more complex and demanding job. There is an acute shortage of professionals who cannot meet the growing needs and auxiliary personnel is one way to meet the increasing demand. Auxiliary personnel would not replace teachers but support them.[4]

Now one American in every 100 workers is employed on a public school institutional staff, serving as a teacher, principal, supervisor, librarian, guidance counselor, special service person, or a consultant. According to a recent National Education Association research report [5] this sudden influx of auxiliary personnel involvement is due to the great advances in all dimensions of life.

Today's teachers must not only be better prepared, but they must also prepare better than their predecessors.

The social, educational, economic and cultural changes have undergone radical changes in the last quarter century. These new dimensions demand that teachers devote their attention exclusively to their professional teaching responsibilities.

---

[4] Ibid.

[5] Estimates of School Statistics, 1967-68, National Education Association Research Report.

It also demands that auxiliary personnel be employed to attend to many of the superficial, time-consuming duties which over-burden teachers. Planned usage of auxiliary personnel is not to replace teachers, but to give them added strength and support so that they may become more proficient and efficient.

Is There a Shortage of Qualified Teachers?

Yes . . . . for all practical purposes there is a serious teacher shortage. Each year 50,000 newly qualified teachers take jobs other than teaching. Each year tens of thousands of practicing teachers leave the schools to marry, to have children, or to enter other occupations. What is called a teacher shortage is therefore, not a shortage of teachers at all, but a shortage of teachers who teach in schools.

For approximately 125,000 teachers, one in every 12 now working in our public schools, this will be their last year in the profession. Probably a third of them will be the best teachers, the best minds, the ones best able to ignite and fan the enthusiasm of their students.

Many will be retiring or leaving for marriage and a family. But too many will quit permanently because they are fed up. Their ambition and self-respect will take them into business or other professions. They will, of course, leave behind a hard core of excellent, dedicated teachers who remain the heart of U.S. education. But they also leave behind an increasing proportion of tired time-savers.

To replace the 125,000 teachers who left last year, only 106,000 college graduates entered the teaching profession. This year 30,000 additional teachers are needed to relieve teaching loads in overcrowded classrooms. [6]

---

[6] Sterling M. McMurrin, edited by, "How We Drive Teachers to Quit," by Richard Meryman, from *Student, School and Society*, 1964, p. 237.

Certain specialist areas are in dire need of immediate relief. More than 2,000 remedial reading teachers are needed to fill present vacancies. Yet, fewer than 200 of these specialists graduate each year from all the nation's colleges according to one informed estimate. [7]

The Honorable Senator Gaylord Nelson stated . . . . despite the mammoth efforts made by the government and educators, students returning to school in the fall of 1967 were met with a national teacher shortage of 72,500 teachers.

It was estimated that in the school year of September 1967, the nation's elementary and secondary schools required 232,400 new teachers while only 63,100 new teachers were expected to graduate from all colleges in 1966, leaving a shortage of 169,300. By 1975 we will need an additional 390,000 teachers in the elementary and secondary schools. A serious teacher shortage is affecting a number of states throughout the nation. [8]

Virtually all teachers basically enjoy teaching and want to excel at their jobs. Many who teach in the nation's thousands of well-run, well-staffed schools really do enjoy it (and excel at it) for years. But the simple truth is that the profession's appeal does not endure long enough for enough teachers.

The average continuous teaching career in U.S. public schools lasts only five years. A survey of a class from the University of Illinois, College of Education, showed that 30% of the class quit after teaching two years, and that 40% did not go into teaching at all, despite their certification. In Utah two years ago, 1,044 (12% of the total) teachers left their jobs. A survey

---

[7] *Staffing for Better Schools*, Office of Education, U.S. Department of Health, Education and Welfare, U.S. Government Printing Office, Division of Printing, Washington, D.C., p. 2.

[8] *Development of Teacher Aide Programs*, U.S. Congressional Record, Vol. 113, Washington, D.C., January 30, 1968, No. 12.

to determine who quit and why they quit showed that one-third of these teachers were rated "very good" and 14% "excellent." The reasons most frequently cited for leaving by "excellent" teachers were working conditions. [9]

Are Teacher Aides Really Needed?

Yes . . . . as Professor Stanley L. Clement recently wrote:

> *"We strive to improve the quality of preparation, yet we ask teachers to perform duties far beneath their level of training . . . . We advocate higher teacher salaries, yet assign our able teachers to tasks that could be done by people with far less ability . . . We seek to raise the professional status of teachers yet keep them performing duties hardly professional . . . . We strive for good teaching morale, yet we keep teachers dissatisfied by requiring them to perform duties which they dislike (but others might enjoy doing). We want teachers to be creative—to experiment, to improve—yet we keep them bored with clerical tasks . . . . It is only common sense to place people at the level of their best talent."* [10]

The teacher is a skilled professional and as such must be permitted to do a professional level of work. He must be a diagnostician and a guider of learning experiences. He should not waste his time on trivia. The utilization of auxiliary personnel can provide the opportunity for teachers to teach.

Superintendents and principals frequently state that contemporary education demands more from educators in both

---

[9] McMurrin, Ibid., p. 238.

[10] Stanley L. Clemet, "Staffing for Better Schools," U.S. Department of Health, Education and Welfare, U.S. Government Printing Office, Division of Printing, Washington, D.C., 1967, p. 14.

their preparation and in their teaching. Therefore, with greater skill demands being placed upon teachers, it is more difficult to find good teachers and hire them.

For the first time, through the use of aides, real opportunity appears for the teacher to provide fresh spontaneity to discussion, to distribute crisply correct tests and syllabi, to investigate new resources and create new materials right in the heart of the school year.[11]

Auxiliary school personnel are a reality, no longer are they an idle dream; they should be sought and respected rather than being a source of hidden fears. They are here because they are needed by the professionals and by the students.

A great number of innovative educational structural changes are the result of trying to overcome staffing problems. The education crisis facing our nation must be met with new and imaginative ideas. The problems created by modern society and technology are new and to deal with them effectively there must be new solutions. Education is confronted with the fierce urgency of now.

Contemporary educational research finds many experimental projects trying to develop new methodologies which will use professional educators more effectively. These projects are probing educational avenues for ways in which teacher aides can be used which will yield a greater number of benefits to both students and instructors.

A major problem yet to be satisfactorily resolved is broadening and increasing a teacher's proficiency and effectiveness through

---

[11] Scott D. Thomson, *The Emerging Role of the Teacher Aide*, The Clearing House, February, 1963, p. 326-30.

relief from certain routine, time-consuming duties. The proper use of teacher aides has the potential for infusing a new and worthwhile perspective in our educational system.

What is the Present Definition of a Teacher Aide?

Educational literature describing teacher aides contains a great deal of conflicting and nondescriptive terminology. Many occupational titles given to persons who are designated to relieve teachers of various sundry tasks are relatively shallow and nebulous. Teacher aides, as an entity and as described in past and contemporary literature, escape any one meaningful definition.

What Definition Should the Title "Teacher Aide" Connote?

Occupational classification titles and job descriptions are as numerous as the imaginative minds devoted to their creation.

The first problem to be resolved is: are we trying to enhance the sub-professional's individual status through the use of a title or is the title to be self-explanatory in describing its possessor?

Terms such as paraprofessional, extending teacher, auxiliary personnel, teacher trainee, and teacher-stretcher are possibly ego-enhancing, but they are also equally confusing terms. These examples of coined terminology are flamboyant and are in reality of relatively little descriptive value.

Superfluous terms escape concrete identification in their whole form and in breaking them down one has a great deal of latitude in choosing from a combination of meanings.

The term "teacher aide" is self-explanatory. This title states the person's occupational status definitely and gives immediate insight into her duties and obligations.

What Should be the Goals of a Teacher Aide Program?

Two basic goals of a teacher aide program should be to serve as an "Adult Out-reach Program" and as a "Student In-reach Program." The program should be structured to provide more child-adult contact within and without both the classroom and the school.

An adult out-reach program could easily serve and provide for many new educative and social services. A program with this orientation could provide for and result in new learning vistas previously unthought of in today's educational system.

The aim of the aide program should decidedly be to help teachers provide and interpret new, better, more meaningful and worthwhile educational insights to the youth entrusted to their care.

Many "ancillary" services could be either initiated or strengthened through a properly planned and administered teacher aide program.

Routine duties designed to free and enhance the instructors' time would be a matter of specific programming for those involved in each team. Assignment of aide duties should be done individually by the supervisor or instructor, and then in accordance with the aide's educational preparation, personal strengths, work experience and willingness to accept specific assignments.

ALL TASKS DELEGATED TO AIDES NEED NOT BE OF A MENIAL NATURE.

What is the Purpose of Teacher Aide Programs?

Generally, the primary purpose of a teacher aide program is to increase the efficiency and effectiveness of teachers in classrooms.

27

Specifically, the purpose of a teacher aide program is at least eleven-fold:

1. To provide a more meaningful and realistic learning situation within any given educational system

2. To make better use of the professional educator's time

3. To provide more time for individual student attention

4. To stress the use of positive education: that of working towards a preventive concept rather than from a remedial concept

5. To allow professional teachers more time to teach or to become more proficient in their specialties

6. To bring about a school-community liaison for understanding

7. To bring about a contiguous factor within the learning process

8. To bring about a greater need for in-depth curriculum planning

9. To create a need for better teacher employment-deployment planning

10. To develop new communication channels and cooperation vistas between teacher-administrator, teacher-teacher, teacher-teacher aide, teacher-pupil and teacher-parent

11. To provide creative and meaningful job opportunities for qualified and interested members of the community.

What is not the Purpose of a Teacher Aide Program?

A teacher aide program is in no way intended to:

1. Reduce or supplant the teaching staff

2. Cut the cost of teaching

3. Endanger teacher salary schedules

4. Downgrade education

5. Usurp the teachers' authority or classroom leadership

6. Force teachers into unwanted or greater teaching loads

7. Force teachers into becoming subject matter specialists

8. Serve as a bargaining benefit in negotiations

9. Evaluate or judge the classroom teacher

10. Provide insignificant and unrealistic jobs, solely to provide employment.

Educators: Are Paraprofessionals (Aides) in Schools to Stay?

Dr. Arnold Glovinsky, director of the Paraprofessional Study, Wayne County, Michigan, Intermediate School District, and Dr. Joseph P. Jones, assistant director of the Paraprofessional Study, Wayne County, Michigan, Intermediate School District, have devised a quiz to test thinking about paraprofessionals.[12] Each statement reflects early findings of the Paraprofessional Study ESEA, Title III, Wayne County Intermediate School District, Detroit, Michigan.

---

[12] Dr. Arnold Glovinsky and Dr. Joseph P. Johns, "A Quiz for Educators," *Nation's Schools*, Vol. 82, No. 2, August, 1968, p. 24.

Before you begin the quiz, one definition is required.

A paraprofessional (aide) is defined as a person who has less than the required or expected level of education or training, but who is performing duties usually performed by the professional under the direct supervision of the certificated person.

A paraprofessional may be a paid or volunteer worker. He may be assigned to assist a teacher, counselor, librarian, or administrator (school-community agent). He may provide general school aid which cuts across rigid position descriptions. In short, a paraprofessional may work in the school or community on tasks, usually performed by the professional or not performed at all.

Correct answers follow. A score of 90 per cent or better — sensational; 70 per cent or better — your perceptions are quite sharp; below 70 per cent — good, you have new worlds to discover.

                                                    YES   NO

1. Virtually all large urban school systems currently employ paraprofessionals.   ____ ____

2. Lack of know-how in the training of paraprofessionals is the chief element preventing growth in the paraprofessional concept.   ____ ____

3. Recently negotiated contracts, which call for duty-free lunch periods for teachers, result in intensified interest in paraprofessional potential.   ____ ____

4. Research indicates that paraprofessionals should be hired to perform only clearly defined tasks.   ____ ____

YES   NO

5. Administrators and teachers soon realize that paraprofessionals can be used to reinforce instruction, to assist in working with boys and girls.   ——— ———

6. Each school or system must decide on what its paraprofessionals should do; there need not be agreement on every aspect of the paraprofessional task.   ——— ———

7. Paraprofessional training must be based on clearly understood *performance goals.* Role must be defined in *behavioral terms.*   ——— ———

8. Paraprofessionals need upward mobility; schools benefit when opportunities for growth on the job are provided.   ——— ———

9. Defining the paraprofessional role forces a redefinition of the teacher role.   ——— ———

10. Paraprofessionals achieve greater effectiveness under the guidance of a central office coordinator specifically assigned to them.   ——— ———

11. Advisory councils facilitate acceptance of paraprofessionals in schools.   ——— ———

12. Sound personnel practice requires a high school diploma as a prerequisite for paraprofessional employment.   ——— ———

13. Officers of professional associations and unions see the influx of paraprofessionals as corrosive to the aims of their organizations.   ——— ———

31

	YES	NO

14. The impact of paraprofessionals in schools will be felt initially at the secondary level. _____ _____

15. Role-playing, self-analysis, games, simulation, small group participation — doing things — are promising training activities for paraprofessionals. _____ _____

16. Teachers must be trained to use paraprofessionals. _____ _____

17. Paraprofessionals provide desirable linkage between school and community. _____ _____

18. Teachers, administrators, community leaders, and paraprofessionals themselves work together to determine the roles of new educational workers. _____ _____

19. Paraprofessionals improve school programs by serving as teacher-counselor-administrator assistants. _____ _____

20. At present the overwhelming support for paraprofessional programs comes from ESEA Title I and OEO funds. _____ _____

Answers

All statements are True except 2, 12, 13 and 14.

2. The chief deterrent is lack of money to pay the salaries of paraprofessionals. The main source of this money today is federal programs. It is likely that increased funds will come from both state and federal sources.

12. A high school diploma is no guarantee that the applicant works well with children. Many excellent candidates will

have to be excluded by such a prerequisite, some of those best qualified. This is particularly the case of indigenous paraprofessionals in inner city schools.

13. On the contrary, when they understand the concept of paraprofessionalism, they view paraprofessionals as enhancing the professional status of teachers.

14. The major impact of paraprofessionalism will be in preschool, elementary, and middle school staffing patterns. Secondary schools will employ paraprofessionals in increased numbers as they become committed to more flexible organizations and programming.

How Widespread is the Use of Teacher Aides?

The Educational Research Service conducted a survey of 217 school systems using teacher aides. The survey indicated 15 school systems used teacher aides only in their secondary schools and 64 systems used aides only at the elementary level.

The remaining 138 school systems reported using teacher aides at both the elementary and secondary levels. The total number of both paid and volunteer aides working in the 217 school systems was 44,351. This figure was broken down to show that approximately 30,000 of these aides were utilized at the elementary level. This figure is not exact for some aides were being used at more than one level.

A further breakdown found that approximately one-third of the 10,000 aides were used with the pre-primary, head-start and kindergarten groups. About one-fourth of the aides worked in the lower primary grades. The remaining 40 per cent of the aides were utilized in the upper elementary grades. There was little difference between the percentage of paid and volunteer aides at each level.

New York City was the largest aide employing system reporting in this survey. This system reported using 9,150 paid aides and 1,850 volunteer aides with 7,475 being used in New York's elementary schools.

Educational Research Service estimated that during the 1965-66 school year the 217 surveyed school systems gave about 400,000 hours of assistance to elementary teachers each week.

The salary rates average about $2.00 per hour. Approximately 25 per cent of the 217 school systems indicated that they relied upon federal funds to pay all teacher aide expenses. Another 25 per cent reported that they relied on funds from local and state revenues. The remaining 50 per cent reported that they used funds from many sources, federal, state, local and private to pay for their teacher aide program.[13]

The New York State Department of Education made a survey of teacher aides in the fall of 1965 [14] which indicated that 428 of the 629 school districts in the state, or 68 per cent, were using teacher aides.

"Of the 428 responding districts now using aides, only 10 have used them in excess of ten years. Twenty-three employed aides for the first time in 1965-66."

"The job assignments of 75 per cent of the aides are in the areas of non-instructional supervisory and clerical duties."[15]

---

[13] *Teacher Aides in Large School Systems,* Educational Research Service Circular, No. 2, 1967, Washington, D.C.; the Association, April, 1967, NEA Stock No. 219-06234.

[14] Ibid.

[15] *Survey of Public School Teacher Aides,* State Education Department, University of the State of New York, Bureau of School and Cultural Research, Albany, The Departmental, April, 1966.

Nearly half of the teacher programs now operating in large public schools are less than three years old. A sampling of large school districts found that 40 per cent of all teacher aide programs were started in the 1965-66 school year and 36 per cent between 1960 and 1964. [16]

Until recently no one has known exactly just how many teachers had the assistance of teacher aides. Today, there are approximately 200,000 aides working in schools throughout the United States. It is estimated that there will be 2,000,000 teacher aides employed by 1975.

A survey by the National Education Research Division (NEA) revealed that one of five public school teachers have some type of teacher aide. Of these, 14 per cent share the services of one or more aides with other teachers, five per cent have the exclusive service of one or more aides. Although the number of aides reported as assisting teachers ranged up to five, very few teachers indicated that they had more than one aide.

Number of Aides	Per Cent of Teachers with Aides Shared	Per Cent of Teachers with Aides Not Shared
More than one	2.5	1.4
One	11.5	3.6
None	86.0	95.0

More than twice as many elementary school teachers (20%) as secondary school teachers (9%) said they were assisted by aides shared with other teachers. The percentage of elementary and secondary teachers who reported having aides on an exclusive basis did not differ significantly. [17]

---

[16] Ibid.

[17] "How the Profession Feels about Teacher Aides," *Teacher Opinion Poll, NEA Journal,* Vol. 56, No. 8, November, 1967, p. 16-17.

All sizes and types of school systems use teacher aides. Researchers find no significant difference between the proportion of teachers in small systems to the proportion in large systems who reported they had teacher aides. It was also determined that geographically more teachers in the west use teacher aides than in any other region of the United States.

A survey of paraprofessionals in the Wayne County schools (Detroit, Michigan) conducted in October, 1967, indicated that of the 43 school districts with 37 responding, 26 school districts reported utilizing paraprofessionals. [18]

The total number of paraprofessionals employed by the district in 1966-67 was 4,839 with 2,579 of the aides being paid. The 1967-68 estimate was 4,904 aides with 2,658 of those aides being paid.

The employment level breakdown level for paraprofessionals in the Wayne County Public Schools for 1966-67 showed that of the 4,839 aides, 2,579 were paid and 625 were employed at the preschool level, 2,979 at the elementary level, 1,015 at the secondary level, and 220 at the adult education level.

Of the 160 non-public schools in Wayne County reporting, 97 reported employment or expected employment of para-professionals during the 1966-67 school year. One hundred-two schools reported expected employment of paraprofessionals for the 1967-68 school year. Of the 160 responding schools, 156 principals expressed an interest in the employment of para-professionals.

Wayne County non-public schools employed 1,582 aides in the 1966-67 school year. Of these, 146 were classified as paid

---

[18] *Paraprofessionalism in the Schools of Wayne County, Michigan,* Report of the Paraprofessional Study, ESEA Title III, Wayne County Intermediate School District, Detroit, Michigan, September, 1968, p. 16-17.

professionals. The upward trend projects employment of 1,718 paraprofessionals with 136 being paid.

For the 1966-67 school year, paraprofessionals in the non-public schools in Wayne County were employed on the following levels: preschool—35, elementary—1,433, secondary—110, and adult education—4.

Total reported use of paraprofessionals in Wayne County for 1966-67, for both public and non-public schools, was 6,421. The estimate for 1967-68 was 6,622 paraprofessionals in Wayne County with 2,725 being paid and 3,696 working as volunteers.

One day auxiliary personnel may outnumber teachers. The trend toward more extensive use of teacher aides is evidenced by the New England Assessment Project which reported that teacher aides have increased in New England (Maine—21%, Connecticut—22%, Massachusetts—46%, New Hampshire—4%, Rhode Island—4%, and Vermont—3%) from 12 school systems employing aides in 1960 to 230 systems in 1967.

Participating in this survey were 1,724 teacher aides. Aides are a significant factor in education in New England and their number will increase as education associations encourage their employment and the federal government provides funds for payment of their salaries through the program. The aides are performing tasks that are ancillary to instruction, thus providing the teacher with more time for preparation and presentation of instructional activities in the classroom. [19]

---

[19] *Teacher Aides in the Classroom*, A Digest, A New England Study Prepared by the New England Educational Assessment Project, A cooperative Regional Report of the Six New England States, Providence, Rhode Island, 1967, p. 8.

What Trends are Developing in the Use of Teacher Aides?

A review of the literature on the employment and deployment of teacher aides reveals the following emerging trends:

A. Teacher aides are becoming more involved in the entire educational process

B. There is a direct correlation between a teacher's proficiency in use of various aide types and the aide's educational involvement and contributions

C. Contemporary teacher aides most often find themselves in blighted urban schools and in high poverty impact areas. Primarily, this may be attributed to the fact that the federal government gives these areas high priority in both service and financial renumeration. Secondly, this is due to the fact that local school systems have trouble enticing and holding good teaching staffs in these areas.

D. Successful teacher aide programs are forcing a structured order

E. Educational institutions are now providing various types of training for teacher aides—without sound guidance criteria. The nebulous nature of teacher aides in the past has aided and abetted the contemporary training confusion. Current trends show emerging formalized programs. Junior Colleges appear to be the chief emerging authority for teacher aides. Junior colleges can and will develop programs that will fit every structured aide category

F. Federal, state, and local governments are becoming more active in their support of teacher aide programs.

Federal, state and local levels hope that through the implementation of sub-professional help:

1. school systems will be able to attract and hold creative and dedicated master teachers

2. a lower teacher-student contact ratio come into existence and achieve a meaningful actuality

3. a greater community-school involvement and rapport will be created through the use of sub-professionals indigenous to the area

4. a teacher aide program will allow more time for individualized adult-student attention

5. educational institutions will stress more positive and preventative methods, rather than propagating present methods which create a demand for remedial educative practices

6. teachers will have time to not only plan their lessons more thoroughly, but also more specifically

7. local educational interests will become community-centered, not just school-centered

8. the sub-professional can and will fill many learning experience voids that are now either being ignored or at best receiving superficial treatment

9. teachers will continue to guard their "territorial rights" with great zeal, especially those who do not fully understand the concepts behind the teacher aide movement

10. teacher aides, like all structured movements, will take steps to improve organization at all levels

11. certain teacher aide categories will be viewed and considered as (rightly so) stepping stones to occupational upgrading

12. teacher training institutions will become more exact in providing their trainees with knowledge to effectively and efficiently use their aides

13. the standard order of college course arrangement will undergo several changes, i.e., Human Growth and Development may come first rather than at the sophomore or junior level. This will also hold true with other disciplines.

14. professional teaching organizations will continue to demand lower teacher-student ratios. The demand has started for teacher aides. Surveys show that if teachers have a choice between either a lower student ratio or a teacher aide, they choose the lower student ratio. Aides are making a great impact on our professional educators and future studies will find teachers choosing an aide over a lower student-teacher ratio.

15. teacher aides will be employed and encouraged in every school system regardless of their poverty or affluence. The teacher aide movement is growing rapidly and from all indications will continue to grow at an ever increasing rate. The teacher aide movement will serve as a great energizing and practical force to allow the teaching profession to become truly professional in every sense of the word.

16. more emphasis will be given to the categorical structuring of aides

17. future aides will be selected for specific needs, rather than qualifications and ability.

CHAPTER II

GOALS AND BENEFITS OF
TEACHER AIDE PROGRAMS

Each generation gives new form to the aspirations that shape education in its time. What may be emerging as a mark of our own generation is a widespread renewal of concern for the quality and intellectual aims of education—but without abandonment of the ideal that education should serve as a means of training well-balanced citizens for a democracy.

Jerome S. Bruner, *The Process of Education* (Cambridge, Mass.: Harvard University Press, 1962) p. 1.

Goals and Benefits of Teacher Aide Programs

Would it be Fair to Assume That a Teacher With a Teacher Aide Will do a Better Job of Teaching?

Yes . . . . . if we believe that many of the time-consuming tasks performed by the teacher do not require a college education. Also, if we believe that the time saved from time-consuming, non-teaching duties will be expended in promoting better teaching.

Educators agree that the effective use of the professional educator's time is an educational imperative. Teachers must be freed from time-consuming, noninstructional duties if a sound educational structure, one that will meet the needs of future students, is to become a reality. They further agree that many contemporary educational practices are outdated and, if not corrected, will be intensified.

A teacher must make use of his aide in an intelligent and professional manner, if he hopes to increase and strengthen his teaching role. Having a teacher aide will not only give a

43

teacher more time to teach and to plan, but it will force the teacher to plan more specifically, realistically and thoroughly. The vast majority of teachers will use the time saved from menial tasks to improve their teaching.

It must be recognized that employment of teacher aides, regardless of how proficient they may be, will not automatically make a poor teacher a good one. Teacher aides are not by design nor purpose expected to be a substitute for a lazy, unimaginative, low-aspiring and unchallenging teacher. However, the proper utilization of teacher aides can prove a valuable innovative device for reshaping and refocusing a teacher's professional image.

Aides can serve as valuable team members, but should seldom serve as the coach and strategist in institutionalized education. As teachers learn to use the various aides effectively, their professional role expectations will automatically change and become more professional.

Change will come only as teacher and administrator see for themselves the actual contributions made by teacher aides. Initially, change will be slow and tedious, but as professionals have more time to be professional and to see the possibilities for utilizing the aides, their enthusiasm will heighten.

The use of aides would allow teachers additional time to take advantage of available information and opportunities, which are necessary for informed decision making and active participation in educational reform.

The aide program has inherent possibilities for truly professionalizing teaching. When teachers are freed from inconsequential and fatiguing responsibilities, they will have greater opportunities to realize their full potential.

Immediate results will generally be slow in coming, but will gradually increase as teachers are able to do more of the activities for which they were trained. Eventually teachers will feel the intrinsic worth and self-fulfillment that directed them to teaching. Less busy work for teachers will give them time to prepare more meaningful assignments which will result in less busy work for the students.

The catalytic value of aides on teachers will free educators from the boredom of monotonous routine and get education off the snail's pace of its present treadmill.

The introduction of teacher aides into our educational structure is one of the most challenging and promising advances in modern education.

A survey by the NEA asked teachers with aides to describe the type of assistance they received from their aides. More than 77 per cent reported help with clerical connected duties, such as recording grades, filing, typing and duplicating; 18 per cent reported more classroom help during recess, bus duty, and lunch. Sixteen per cent reported aides assisting in large group instruction such as music, art, lay reading, marking and grading papers. Another 14 per cent reported aide assistance with small group or individual instruction related to reading, spelling, etc. Thirteen per cent reported aide assistance in the preparation and use of instructional resources, and nine per cent with jobs related to classroom environment such as housekeeping duties with some classroom monitoring.

The secondary teachers reported that their aide assistance was 86 per cent clerical, as compared with 73 per cent for elementary teachers.

Teachers who reported that they were assisted by aides were asked to evaluate this assistance. An overwhelming majority (9 in 10 teachers) indicated that having teacher aides was helpful, and more than half said that it was a *great* assistance.

Assistance	Total	Elementary	Secondary
Clerical	77.6%	73.0%	85.9%
With non-classroom duties	18.4	24.7	7.1
With large group	15.9	16.3	15.2
With small group or individual instruction	13.7	18.5	5.1
With preparation and use of instructional resources	13.4	15.7	9.1
With classroom environment	8.6	10.7	5.1
Other	0.7	1.1	0.0

Teachers in the small school systems were the most enthusiastic about the assistance provided by their aides.[1]

	Total	Large	Medium	Small
Great Assistance	51.4%	49.3%	47.9%	58.6%
Some Assistance	38.4%	34.3%	41.4%	36.8%
Little Assistance	9.5%	13.4%	10.7%	4.6%
No Assistance	0.7%	3.0%	0.0%	0.0%

In answer to this question, it would be safe to assume that an intelligent, imaginative, efficient, and ambitious teacher's talent would be much more productive with sub-professional help to care for the routine chores. Without the above qualities, it is doubtful that teacher aides would enhance the teacher's proficiency to any substantial degree.

What Effect Will Increased Teacher Aide Personnel Have on the Teaching Profession?

The planned and effective use of auxiliary personnel could prove to be one of the most significant advances in education. As teachers learn to use the released time from their endless

---

[1] "How the Profession Feels About Teacher Aides," *Teacher Opinion Poll, NEA Journal*, Vol. 56, No. 8, November, 1967.

essential but inconsequential chores, their professional lives will take on new perspectives. Teachers will be able to devote more time to teaching and be able to assume a more professional role. New organizational structuring and planning will evolve from national to local levels. Teacher involvement will increase with new roles developing for both the teachers and the teacher aides. The successful implementation of a teacher aide program will cause ramifications which will effect every segment of the present educational structure. Teacher training institutions will need to take into account, make allowances and preparations for this growing personnel dimension in education. It is possible that aide-intern service may become a regular part of teacher preparations.

The experience a new teacher gains from her internship as an aide will help her to better utilize the aide she is assigned. The internship will also give her experience that will enable her to be a better teacher.

Aide-internship would also force colleges and schools to work together more closely in matters of planning, staffing, and evaluation.

Is an Increase in Classroom Enrollment the Primary Aim in Employing Teacher Aides?

No, the primary aim in hiring teacher aides is to increase or enhance quality education.

A sample of teachers were asked whether they thought they would be more effective teaching classes of 25 to 30 pupils and taking care of the non-teaching duties themselves, or teaching classes of 40 to 50 pupils with a full-time aide assisting with non-teaching duties. Five in six teachers or 84% answered that they believed they would be more effective teaching the smaller group and taking care of all non-teaching duties.

A larger proportion of elementary teachers (88%) than of secondary teachers (79%) believed that the smaller classes were more essential to effective teaching than a full-time aide.[2]

For those communities unwilling to financially underwrite the potential of an aide program, single teachers or teams of teachers can be found who will gladly accept a slightly heavier pupil load as compensation for assistance. If six teachers accept two additional students per class period, an aide's salary is paid.

However, most teachers agree that any aide plan that offers any promise of relieving the overburdened teachers from non-educational or non-classroom duties will be embraced by the teachers with a normal class load but not by those teachers who will be faced with a load increase. The aim in employing teacher aides is not to justify a heavier class load but to enhance the educational benefits of a normal class size.

Will the Addition of Teacher Aides Make Teachers Less Aware of Student Needs?

Neglect of student needs could occur, but only if the teachers allow it to happen. There is no safeguard against this happening with or without an aide in the classroom. The success or failure of any classroom endeavor rests largely upon the leadership of the teacher. Traditionally, the operation of the classroom is the function of the teacher. Therefore, no amount of standardization, centralization, or supervision alone, even if so intended, could dogmatically and arbitrarily impersonalize the instructional process. It is a teachers professional responsibility to remain alert and attentive to the student's needs.

---

[2] "How the Profession Feels About Teacher Aides," *Teacher Opinion Poll, NEA Journal*, Vol. 56, No. 8, November, 1967.

Ideally, an aide should serve as an additional and active resource in keeping the teacher conscious of student needs. Furthermore, teachers with aides have the advantage of another adult observer who can give them insight, opinions and advice.

Can the Utilization of Auxiliary Personnel Provide the Opportunity for Teachers to Teach?

To answer this question we must first assume the basic premise that all baccalaureate degree teachers are proficiently skilled and professionally oriented educators, actively seeking greater sophistication. Secondly, we must further assume that teachers do become more proficient if allowed to work in a professional and challenging environment with menial educational trivia being taken care of by an aide.

Where the above-outlined premises prove positive, each teacher's educational impact would be greater and more beneficial to their students. Too much of a teacher's time is wasted on essential but inconsequential chores. The teacher's job has become overburdened with non-teaching duties. Teachers stand alone among professional people in the volume of nonprofessional work they are required to do.

Practitioners in every professional field dealing with groups of people or with complex operations have auxiliary helpers: doctors have nurses, and they in turn have nurses' aides, dentists have dental technicians, lawyers have legal secretaries and law clerks, researchers have specialists and assistants, college professors have various helps in graders, readers, proctors and assistants, and business executives have executive secretaries and administrative assistants.

Every moment a teacher spends in encroaching, noninstructional phases of his position, reduces the amount of time he has to spend on the real job for which he was hired—teaching. A poll taken of 206 teachers, of whom approximately half had used aides and half had not, indicated that an overwhelming majority of all teachers agree that the use of an aide permits the teachers to do more teaching.[3]

Teaching aides in the past have most often been relegated to performing minor superficial chores. Whatever aid and comfort they provided the teachers was for the most part appreciated. However, being of an unstructured and sporadic nature, teacher aides at best gave only partial relief.

Therefore, all teacher aides, regardless of their occupational category or involvement, should be required to undergo at least basic indoctrination covering their specific roles, duties and obligations. The effectiveness and success of a teacher aide program will be in direct proportion to the cooperation and understanding found between the teacher and his aide.

Only as professionals are freed to be more professional, only as they witness the reliability of teaching aides, will headway be made in the destruction of prevailing myths and prejudices.

The aim of the teacher aide program is better education for every child. The introduction of aides into schools has strengthened analysis of schools and self-analysis of teachers. Since teachers realize that they must clarify their own goals and practices before they can interpret them to their helpers, this yields a better presentation in the classroom to students.

The use of aides in various capacities has yielded a new source of manpower for school officials and new patterns of staff utilization. In addition, they are creating exciting auxiliary positions in school programs and new job opportunities for citizens in their communities.

---

[3] *A Cooperative Study for the Better Utilization of Teacher Competencies*, Final Evaluation Report, An Evaluation Report Prepared by an Outside Evaluating Committee, Central Michigan University, Mt. Pleasant, Michigan, 1958, p. 27.

To What Extent Can Teacher Aides Free the Teacher's Time to Teach?

The amount of time freed for each teacher to use for teaching will depend basically on the individual teacher's ingenuity. The secret of freed teacher time rests in the degree of sophistication and resourcefulness used by each teacher in the assignment and deployment of aides.

In one research study it was found that a typical teacher can spend:

89% less time - correcting papers
83% less time - monitoring written lessons
76% less time - taking the role
61% less time - moving groups of pupils around
36% less time - disciplining pupils
25% less time - preparing reports

And that a typical teacher would now have:

105% more time - to prepare lessons
57% more time - to hear recitations
41% more time - to supervise activities such as art
27% more time - to help individual pupils at their desks
20% more time - to make and explain lesson assignments [4]

What Benefits Have Resulted From the Teacher Aide Program?

The Bank Street College of Education in New York conducted a study on the effectiveness of aides in 15 pilot programs scattered

---

[4] "To What Extent Can Teacher Aides Free The Teacher's Time To Teach?" *U.S. News and World Report*, May 11, 1956.

across the United States.[5] The results of the study give credence to other recent research projects that indicate that teacher aides provide education with several positive factors.

Positive advantages of the programs are:

1. Aides frequently seek new, challenging educational experiences.

2. Aides attain a renewed self-respect and develop a more positive outlook on life.

3. Teachers tend to become more proficient in their instructional and professional activities.

4. Teachers become more involved and tend to experiment in curriculum and staff planning.

5. There is a tendency toward greater lay citizen involvement in school activities and functions.

6. Aides serve as a recruitment inducement.

7. Students tend toward slightly higher academic achievement when there is an aide in the classroom.

8. Activities tend to become student-directed rather than text oriented.

Some unanticipated by-products[6] which have resulted in connection with the Teacher Aide program are:

1. Disciplinary problems have decreased because of the consistency of one authority figure in dealing with cafeteria and playground problems.

---

[5] Garda W. Bowman and Gordon J. Klopf, "New Careers and Roles in the American School." A study conducted for the Office of Economic Opportunity, New York: Bank Street College of Education, September, 1967, p. 36-37, p. 153-154.

[6] Revision of the article, "The How for Teachers Who Will Be Using Teacher Aides for the First Time," Central Michigan College, Mt. Pleasant, Michigan, 1958.

2. High staff turnover, as a result of large classes, problem students, or work loads, may be decreased.

3. The unique competences of some of the aides have provided unusual enrichment opportunities for pupils.

4. The public relations program of the school has, in many instances, been improved by the addition of lay persons as aides to the school staff.

5. Greater use of instructional aids, devices, and materials has resulted through the use of teacher aides. In many instances, the aides have learned to operate equipment which teachers were unable or reluctant to use before.

6. A high percentage of those who are employed as aides become interested in teaching and enroll in courses leading toward certification and degrees.

7. Aide use tends to motivate and upgrade teacher achievement in the classroom.

8. The aide provides another set of eyes and ears for the teacher.

9. Aides assert their work at school has helped them to be more patient with children in their own homes; they feel more tolerant with their own children and better understand the value of time spent with them.

10. Aides discover that children from large families and in large classes seldom had an adult with whom they could talk and who is willing to listen to them as individuals.

The school is seen as an instrument for social change and the classroom is the place where parents, as aides, and teachers can actively alter each others' perceptions, attitudes and behaviors.

CHAPTER III

VOLUNTEER OR PAID AIDES?

Educational values should reflect general cultural values, bolster them at weak points, and help maintain balance in their interplay. They provide a standard for present practices and a guide for future ones.

Richard I. Miller, *Education in a Changing Society* (Washington, D.C.: National Education Association, 1963), p. 9.

Volunteer or Paid Aides?

What Should be the Definition of a Volunteer Teacher Aide?

A volunteer teacher aide should be defined as: Any person engaged by a school system, who voluntarily devotes time to the performance of various duties, either within or without the classroom, as agreed upon by legally responsible, educational supervisory personnel.

What Should be the Definition of a Paid Teacher Aide?

A paid teacher aide should be defined as: Any person within a school system who is legally and specifically employed to assist certified teachers in the discharging of their teaching and ancillary duties and is paid for their services.

Why Favor Paid Teacher Aides Over Volunteer Aides?

For any educational program to have value and merit it must be planned and have direction, goals and discipline in its make-up.

If teacher aides are paid, the employing school has the responsibility to set up and to maintain policies and regulations with the right to command adherence to the agreed-upon conditions of employment.

Paid aides are a part of the school staff and enjoy the guaranteed rights and benefits of a paid position. Hence, the employing school can demand and expect the same degree of conformity, responsibility, cooperation and punctuality it demands from all employees.

In the United States, education is big business. Taking a quick lesson from the school of business, one quickly learns that business growth does not rely on nor is it the result of volunteer labor.

In most cases volunteer aides are at best only a stopgap measure that is erratic, confusing and unpredictable and often creates situations untenable to all involved.

The use of supervised student aides may be an exception to the above. A case can be made for scattered individualized programs using volunteer aides but, by and large, a volunteer aide program is inferior to a paid aide program.

What Does the Paid Teacher Aide Program Need in Order to Become an Integral Part of the Educational Process?

If paid teacher aides are to become an integral part of the educational process they must have legitimate and recognized status. Before an aide legitimizing process can be solidly undertaken educators must resolve a basic question: "Is teaching a profession?"

If this is affirmed, next in order of importance is to take several good long hard looks at the so-called critical areas in the educational process, to see what implications, innovations, or alterations are needed to enhance and upgrade the entire educational process. If teaching is truly a profession, educators must view it as such and move as a dynamic innovative force within a dedicated sense of purpose and direction for teaching, not just school-keeping. Contemporary action often finds fractionated masses reacting negatively with unprofessional and selfish interests serving as the motivating stimuli.

What is a Typical Paid Aide?

Paid aides, like volunteer aides are men, women, and students, of all ages, from all walks of life, who are hired to perform specific, designated functions in a school system.

The profile of a typical paid teacher aide would indicate that she is: a female, working more than 20 hours a week, serving more than one teacher, working in a range of levels from pre-kindergarten through the upper elementary. She has a high school education and earns approximately $2.00 per hour, which most often comes from federal resources. Generally, she has been recommended for employment by someone within or connected to the school system. She has passed an initial screening, necessary because of a surplus of job applicants. She has also passed some sort of physical health examination.

Usually she has been training through a series of conferences with her immediate supervisor or supervisors, and possibly in a specially initiated in-service workshop designed for aides.

More than 80% of her time is spent on bookkeeping, house-keeping, storekeeping and clerical functions, with less than 10% of her time being spent in exposure to the classroom environment.

59

Should Paid Aides be Employed Full- or Part-Time?

All teacher aide employment should be predicated on planned deployment, with the use of aides varying from school to school. Factors determining employment and time involvement are:

1. Community acceptance
2. School board acceptance
3. School administration acceptance
4. Local teacher association acceptance
5. The determined needs of the school
6. Budgetary allowance
7. The type and availability of personnel.

Primarily, the types of teacher aides to be used will determine the hours of employment.

If part-time clerical aides are the only type aide used, hours of employment could be determined by a planned workable schedule.

In the case of classroom teaching aides, full-time employment is most desirable for two basic reasons: (1) they can identify themselves with the school more easily and (2) they can more easily be identified as an integral part of the educational program. Practicality and quality should be the guiding criteria resolving this question of hours of employment.

Will Paid Teacher Aide Programs Cost the School Systems More Money?

Presently, the answer to this question is "yes." Initially, the employment of teacher aide personnel will require increased expenditures by local school systems. Federal legislation has been passed which gives financial consideration to schools for the employment of teacher aides.

Federal legislation for teacher aides is predicated on five basic factors:

1. It allows more meaningful employment.

2. It serves as an encouraging step to individuals seeking occupational upgrading.

3. It allows educational institutions to better meet contemporary student needs.

4. It emphasizes a positive or preventive approach more desirable than the remedial program.

5. In long-range planning, good education costs less per student than poor education.

As teacher aide programs are rapidly expanding, local school districts are committing more of their operating funds to this practice. Funds are not only being spent on aide employment but also on continued aide training.

Presently, federal monies are given only to help the lower socio-economic children. This practice will eventually fade as it is realized that it is unrealistic, restrictive and detrimental to the overall educational system.

Reimbursable programs such as head-start, upward bound, and teacher aides should be available to all students of proven educational need, regardless of their economic standing. The practice of using fixed incomes as the determining criteria for the degree of needed educational services is as archaic as it is unrealistic and it borders on ignorant professional malpractice.

Future legislation and financial appropriations will be predicated on the program's acceptance of its overall success.

In Minneapolis, 244 aides worked a 15-hour week, with one hour a week devoted to in-service training, in 28 schools last year. Forty-one schools are involved in this year's program with 400 aides participating so far. Local school monies are also being used this year for the first time.

St. Paul schools originally funded their aide program solely out of local tax monies. Federal monies were used to hire an additional 200 aides in 1965 to augment the 50 previously on the job. The program has been greatly expanded for 1966-67 school year, with increases in both local and federal money available. Total number of aides participating in the St. Paul program in both public and parochial elementary and secondary schools is 287 for this year. '

In judging costs, the time factor must be taken into consideration. Short-range educational planning will find a paid teacher aide program will increase the per-pupil educational cost. The reasons for the additional costs are the same as those found in all short-range programs. Time is an economizing factor in program costs. Long-range educational planning will find that the paid aide program will decrease the overall, per-pupil educational cost.

New methods and improvement in any area generally involve higher costs. Although money is a prime factor and an expediter of miracles, the initial cost outlay should not be the sole dictator of the merits of a teacher aide program. The most important question is whether the advantages gained from paid teacher aides are worth the additional cost. This can be judged on the basis of these two questions:

1. Will teacher aides prevent waste of time, money, and resources which occurs when professional teachers are encumbered and/or prevented from fully developing and maximizing their potential?

' Betty Wilcox, "What is the Teacher Aide's Role," *Minnesota Journal of Education*, May, 1967.

2. Will the use of aides bring about conditions more conducive to better teaching, greater educational benefits to the student-teacher relationships, and a lower rate of teacher turnover?

How are Teacher Aides Rewarded?

Four basic factors must be considered in determining remuneration for teacher aides:

> the type of aide
> the hours of employment
> the conditions of employment
> the type of deployment.

Student aides are rewarded in a number of ways:

> by an enriching experience
>
> as fulfillment of a service club or future teachers club task assignment
>
> as a means of working out school fees
>
> as a unit credit towards graduation, usually one-half unit of credit each semester with an allowable maximum of two full unit credits
>
> at a paid hourly rate, generally minimal.

Volunteer aides are rewarded basically with the personal satisfaction they derive from giving service and help to youth and the heartfelt "thank you" of the students and teachers.

Special aides may receive all types of remuneration, including command of the highest teacher aide financial benefits. The salary range for special aides at this time is between $2.00 and $5.00 per classroom hour.

Practical aides and certified aides at the present time (except for isolated cases) show no remunerable differentials between these two aide types. The minimum figure for these aides is $1.25 per hour with the maximum at $2.60 per hour. The New York State Teachers Association's survey showed the median hourly pay rate for the New York City area to be $2.25 per hour as compared to upstate New York where the median hourly rate was $1.67 per hour.

This study gives support to the commonly held supposition that higher pay is available in larger cities. In spot checking other metropolitan districts as compared to outlying districts, the same pay policy differentials are found. In Michigan the scale ranged from $1.25 to $3.50 per hour with the hourly average at approximately $1.80 per hour. The wages paid aides in Wayne County Public Schools (Detroit area) ranged from a minimum hourly rate of $1.25 to a maximum hourly rate of $3.50 and a minimum yearly rate of $1,500 to a maximum yearly rate of $3,520. This area employed 4,839 paraprofessionals in the 1966-67 school year with 2,574 being paid. The estimated employment figure for 1967-68 was 4,904 with 2,658 being paid. [2]

Although programs vary, a typical local program may follow along lines similar to those of the Altoona, Pennsylvania schools as reported for their 1966 teacher aide program and its nature of pay.

The program employed 40 practical aides at $1.25 per hour for aides in training for the first 40 days, $1.35 per hour for the next 40 days, and $1.50 per hour for the remainder of the school term. Upon successful completion of the training, the trainee is hired on a permanent basis at $1.75 per hour.

---

[2] *The Practice and the Promise*, Paraprofessionalism in the schools of Wayne County, Michigan, Report of the Paraprofessional Study, ESEA Title IV, Wayne County Intermediate School District, Detroit, Michigan, September, 1968.

To determine successful completion of the training program, candidates are rated on a five point scale: skill, use of the English language, personality, poise and appearance.

When hired, aides work a six hour day and perform their duties only while the students are in school. [3]

The New England Educational Assessment research project of 1,724 teacher aides reported that of the school systems replying, 78% were paying teacher aides less than a substitute teacher, 10% the same as a substitute teacher and 7% more than a substitute teacher. Salaries usually reflect educational background. [4]

Reader-grader aides are often paid on a piecework scale type operation. The rates vary considerably according to the area of employment. The reader-grader aide program has met with greater success than envisioned or even hopefully anticipated a few years ago. Testimonials giving acclaim and accolades to the reader-grader aide programs can be summoned throughout the United States.

Per page rates for reader-grader aides range from $.15 to $.35. This cost is subject to prevailing area wage rates and also the length and type of paper figure in determining per page cost.

Hourly rates are generally preferred over the piecework method by many educators for various personal and professional reasons.

The hourly rate is generally set at a minimum of $1.50 with a maximum of $3.50—over $3.50 is considered an exception.

---

[3] John J. Branick, "How to Train and Use Teacher Aides," *Phi Delta Kappan*, October, 1966, Vol. XLVIII, No. 2.

[4] *Teacher Aides in the Classroom*, A Digest, A New England Study Prepared by the New England Educational Assessment Project, A Cooperative Regional Report of the Six New England States, Providence, Rhode Island, 1967, p. 8.

In addition to this, the reader-grader aide can be used as a resource tutor or for conferences. The rates for these two services range from $2.00 to $5.00 per hour. The advanced training and screening requirement for reader-grader aides accounts for the greater wage differential.

Past experience has indicated that because teacher aide salaries have not been contracted or stabilized, they often have been set at hourly rates ranging from $1.25 to $4.00 per hour depending on the economic standing of the particular school district. It is desirable that whenever possible the aide should be placed on a salary schedule commensurate with other hourly rated employees in the school district, and no higher. Too often an inconsistency in salaries, especially among staff members build up to insurmountable barriers.

Some school districts have placed their aides on annual contracts, while others are strictly hourly. The most stable situation appears to be one where an aide is committed to work each day that school is in session for the length of the school day. Generally speaking this would amount to 30 hours per week for 10 months with time off during the normal school year (Thanksgiving, Christmas, Easter, etc.).

In February of 1969 the Union School District in Jackson, Michigan, which employs 50 teacher aides, gave the aide classifications the same fringe benefit package given to maintenance, custodial and cafeteria personnel.[5]

This package included:

a. a fully paid hospitalization insurance program for aides and their families

---

[5] Clarence Lacny, Utilizing Teacher Aides in the Jackson, Michigan, Public Schools, "A Dual Opportunity," Jackson Public Schools, 1970.

b. a $2,000 term life insurance policy

c. one paid sick day per month for each month of employment, cumulative to 90 days

d. five paid vacation days per year.

Although teacher aide personnel did not join either of the unions representing the maintenance, custodial and cafeteria personnel, they were arbitrarily placed in this group by school administrators to avoid a third negotiating force.

The Jackson Public Schools teacher aide salary schedule is as follows:

Classi-fication	Pay Basis	Minimum 1st yr.	Next Year	Next Year	Next Year	Maximum 5th year	8 yrs. Total 1 yr. at Max.	15 yrs. Total & 1st Rate
5	Hourly	$1.99	$2.08	$2.18	$2.28	$2.39	$2.50	$2.63
7	Hourly	2.18	2.28	2.39	2.50	2.62	2.74	2.88
8	Hourly	2.28	2.39	2.50	2.62	2.74	2.88	3.02
9	Hourly	2.39	2.50	2.62	2.74	2.88	3.00	3.15

Teacher Aide classifications are:

5 Teacher-Aide I — Non-High School Graduate

7 Teacher-Aide II — High School Graduate and up to 60 semester hours of college credit

(7) (Matron Attendant for Special Education)

8 — High School Graduate and Teacher Aide Certificate from Jackson Community College

9 Teacher Assistant — More than 60 semester hours of college credit

Fringe benefits are included for all these classifications.

The teacher aide movement is rapidly becoming a recognized force on the educational scene. Now is the time for individual teachers, professional organizations and school administrators to realize the inherent value and potential of aides. Professional educators must provide the structures, establish order, create acceptance, and make provisions for the employment, training and utilization of the aides.

Teacher Aides Are Here Because They Are Needed.

How are Teacher Aides Being Received by Administrators and Teachers?

In 1965 a study conducted by the New York State Education Department[6] indicated that 428 of 629 school districts in the state were employing 3,134 teacher aides. Ninety-three per cent of the districts considered their experience with aides favorable. Twenty-six districts were neutral while only four expressed unfavorable opinions. Dissenting opinion seemed to appear heavily in noninstructional supervisory areas where responsibility was mainly in the lunchroom. [7]

Reissman and Pearl[8] cite a favorable experiment in a team-teaching project which began in Pittsburgh in 1960. Twenty mothers were recruited to assist in duplicating prepared material, operating audio-visual equipment, and performance of other related tasks. The project was so successful that the number of aides was doubled after the first four years.

---

[6] *Survey of Public School Teacher Aides*, State Education Department, University of the State of New York, Bureau of School and Cultural Research, Albany, The Departmental, April, 1966.

[7] Ibid.

[8] Frank Reissman and Arthur Pearl, *New Careers for the Poor*, New York: Free Press, 1965.

A survey by the NEA Research Division [9] revealed that almost one in five public school teachers (19%) has the assistance of a teacher aide. Of these, 14% share the services of one or more aides with other teachers, 5% have one or more aides for their services exclusively.

This survey included all teachers, regardless of whether or not they had teacher aides. The survey described three types of duties and asked the teachers whether they were in favor of or against assistance by an aide. The three types of duties were:

1. Certain types of classroom instruction, e.g., conducting reading groups, running audio-visual equipment, etc.

2. Grading and marking papers.

3. Clerical duties, e.g., typing tests, filling report cards, etc.

A substantial majority of teachers (84%) said they would like assistance with clerical duties. Teachers were about evenly divided between those who would like assistance in grading and marking papers (51%) and those who would prefer to do this themselves (49%). More than half the teachers that were questioned (56%) reported that they would rather perform all duties related to classroom instruction themselves. [10]

Having more teacher aides is no substitute for having more teachers, according to respondents. Some persons have proposed that teacher aides be used to enable qualified teachers to instruct larger classes of pupils, but teachers in general disagree.

---

[9] "How the Profession Feels About Teacher Aides," *Teacher Opinion Poll. NEA Journal*, Vol. 56, No. 8, November, 1967.

[10] Ibid.

Because of some teacher resistance and administrative problems, not everyone applauds teacher aides, but most school-men surveyed find that teacher aides are a worthwhile contribution in the classroom.

How do Teachers Feel About Spending Money for Teacher Aides?

The first question that teachers will usually ask when talking about a teacher aide program for the first time is, "Which duties are teacher aides expected to perform?" This is usually followed by the question, "Where, what and whose money will be used to pay teacher aide salaries?" If the money to support this program is coming from federal or private sources, teachers are more likely to answer affirmatively than if it is to come out of local operating revenues.

In a National Commission on Teacher Education and Professional Standards Study on Auxiliary School Personnel, the National Education Association [11] found that generally teachers do not think that the development of a teacher aide program should have financial priority over the improvement of professional salaries. However, teachers agree that they would favor the school system investing in an aide program.

To obtain these reactions, the following question was asked: "Suppose your school system had in next year's budget an additional sum equal to $500 per teacher and was deciding among three options for the best allocation of this money. Which option would you prefer?

---

[11] "How the Profession Feels About Teacher Aides," *Teacher Opinion Poll, NEA Journal*, Vol. 56, No. 8, November, 1967.

1. Use all of the money to increase teacher salaries.

2. Use all of the money to employ part-time teacher aides.

3. Use half the money to increase teacher salaries and half to employ part-time aides."

Forty-eight percent of the teachers favored dividing the money between teacher salaries and an aide program. Forty percent favored allocating the entire sum to teacher salaries and twelve percent said that the entire amount ought to be allocated to financing teacher aides.

Substantially more secondary teachers favored allocating all the additional funds to the increase of teacher salaries than did elementary teachers.

	Total	Elementary	Secondary
All for salaries	40.4%	33.7%	47.9%
All for aides	11.5%	14.0%	8.8%
Equal division of funds	48.0%	53.3%	43.3%

The preference for aides at the elementary level can be partially explained by the heavy emphasis teacher aides are receiving at the elementary level while they are relatively new at the secondary level.

Many master contracts are now containing provisions for the inclusion of teacher aides. The teacher aide salary question will continue to be a point of contention in bargaining, but it will not reach the point of being an exclusive factor.

CHAPTER IV

LEGAL STATUS AND RESPONSIBILITY
OF TEACHER AIDES

Today's society is so complex that it is difficult not to be overcome by the responsibility for understanding it—Particularly, understanding it to the point of being able to interpret its needs correctly and to plan educational programs appropriate to those needs.

Dorothy Neubauer (Ed.), *Contemporary Society: Background for the Instructional Program* (Washington, D.C.: National Education Association, 1957), p.7.

Legal Status and Responsibility of Teacher Aides

What are the Legal Responsibilities of Teacher Aides?

Teacher aides, regardless of their employment or deployment capacity, whether paid or unpaid, should adhere to all the legal requirements applicable to any other school employees.

> When teacher aides are assigned tasks involving supervision, they are placed in positions of potential liability for pupil injury. In such a situation, liability is likely to arise out of negligence on the part of the aide. Any person assigned such responsibilities is ignorant at his own peril. If he is not qualified to supervise playgrounds, etc., he should not try to do so.

> In cases involving pupil injury the courts have traditionally held the teacher to a higher standard of care than that owed to the general public. Likewise, a teacher aide when placed in a supervisory capacity owes the

pupils a greater standard of care than is normally required in other personal relationships. [1]

Legal questions and actions regarding torts should never be an issue if aides perform their duties under the general supervision of a legally certified educator. However, precautionary measures must be considered and practiced. Every action performed by school personnel must be predicated on sound judgment and substantiated by the use of reasonable care and prudence.

What is the Legal Employment Status of Teacher Aides?

Because most states do not have specific statutory provisions pertaining to teacher aides, there have been instances in which the power of school boards has been challenged. However, judicial authority has generally supported the premise that, in the absence of statutes to the contrary, the power to hire and pay teacher aides is within the authority of local school districts.

In a Minnesota legal battle over the employment of a school nurse the court said:

> "The purpose of the corporation is to maintain efficient free public schools . . . and, unless expressly restricted, (the school board) necessarily possesses the power to employ such persons as are required to accomplish the purpose." [2]

Other courts have held that the board has the authority to determine the mode and course of instruction.

---

[1] S. Kern Alexander, "What Teacher Aides Can-And Cannot—Do," *Nation's Schools*, Vol. 82, No. 2, August, 1968.

[2] *State v. Brown*, 112 minn., 370, 128 N.W., p. 294.

To avoid the challenged power some state legislatures have recently enacted statutes providing for the employment of teacher aides. Not all statutes are comprehensive and explicitly detailed but they do give the employment of teacher aides a legal basis. In other states, state boards of education and state departments of education have released statements specifying the use of aides in the public schools. These statements do not carry the weight of law, but they do imply direction and guidance in the employment and deployment of teacher aides.

Giving legal sanction to the aide program are legislatively enacted programs such as the Elementary and Secondary Education Act of 1965 which provides many school districts with the necessary funds to employ teacher aides to assist in programs designed for culturally deprived children.

The Education Professions Development Act provides pre-service or in-service training of aides which will enable them to be better aides. In order to participate in this program the state must have a designated program of state supervision and leadership for the development of policies and procedures on the use of federal funds to obtain and train teacher aides. [3]

Each state has its specific certification laws which specifically state the minimal qualifications for persons before they may become teachers in the schools. Therefore, unless there are specific statutes providing for other means, a teacher aide is not authorized to perform instructional duties or to teach. [4]

---

[3] *Guide for Preparing a State Plan for Attracting and Qualifying Teachers to Meet Critical Teacher Shortages*, Part B, subpart 2, of the Education Professions Development Act (Title V of the Higher Education Act of 1965).

[4] Kentucky, O.A.C., No. 269-1963.

Are Supervisors, Administrators and School Districts Liable for the Negligent Actions of a Teacher Aide?

Three basic precautions will reduce the liability factor in the employment and utilization of teacher aides:

1. School districts, administrators and supervisors should be certain that proper and adequate aide selection criteria has been established and is being followed.

2. All aide types employed should be aware of and be prepared to accept the responsibilities of their job. An orientation session should take place before the assumption of any major employment responsibilities. The initial orientation should pertain to the duties undertaken and acquaintance with the operation of the school, with stress being placed on their responsibilities to students, teachers, school, and community.

3. Serious consideration must be given to proper aide placement.

If these three factors are conscientiously applied the school districts, administrators and supervisors will not be held liable for negligence on the part of the aide. This opinion is based on the generally accepted practice of not holding school districts, administrators or supervisors in public schools responsible or liable for any commissions or omissions on the part of their personnel, if adequate precautions have been taken.

If school districts, administrators or supervisors assign duties to teacher aides for which the aide is not qualified, they may be held responsible for the negligent actions of the aide.

CHAPTER V

INITIATING THE PROGRAM

From many parts of the country come reports of ways in which schools are trying to improve the quality of their educational programs by bringing organizational patterns into closer alignment with goals and activities.

Mary Dawson (Ed.), *Elementary School Organization* (Washington, D.C.: National Elementary Principal, 1961), p. 4.

Initiating the Program

What Can National, State and Local Professional Teacher Organizations do to Help Teacher Aide Programs Get Started?

Professional groups and associations can be involved in the original conceptualization as well as in continuing program development of teacher aide programs. To insure success of a teacher aide program, there must be coordinated action at the state and local levels of the professional organizations and school systems which will promote mutual understanding and provide for compromise on conflicting issues and views.

A broad cross section of professionals involved in the formulation of guidelines and the setting of requirements will insure a diversity of ideas and opinions which will avoid exploitation of auxiliary personnel as well as protecting the teachers and pupils from abuse. A diversity of opinions will also provide encouragement for the needed leeway for experimentation.

The most eminent problem challenging teacher aide programs today is that of professional opposition. Teachers who "know" that the outcome of an experimental teacher aide program will not be worthwhile, even before the project has been implemented, are not displaying the open-mindedness expected of all good teachers.

Generally, the objecting personnel are those who have never considered a personnel structure different from the one which is prevalent. [1]

Illustrating this feeling are the hostile reactions of teacher organizations in Bay City, Michigan, to the teacher aide program. Teacher organizations should be the first to propose and support such projects, yet the negative attitude toward the very idea of experimentation in Bay City has been rather poorly disguised as criticism of the research design and the alleged results of the Bay City project. [2]

The National Commission on Teacher Education and Professional Standards sees the addition of auxiliary personnel in the schools as one of the most challenging and hopeful advances in modern education. [3]

Professional organizations have the duty to insure that programs be cooperatively planned by school systems, institutions of higher learning, professional staffs and organizations. It should be their responsibility to insure a comprehensive, continuing, in-depth program of development and supervision

---

[1] Myron Lieberman, *The Future of Public Education*, Phoenix Books, The University of Chicago Press, Chicago, Illinois, 1967, p. 100.

[2] Ibid.

[3] *Auxiliary School Personnel*, National Commission on Teacher Education and Professional Standards, National Education Association, 1967.

of aide programs by providing open-ended employment opportunities which insure that the level of responsibility is balanced with available training.

Professional organizations can also serve as a quality control function by aiding in assessment of aides, by defining qualifications for aides as related to specific subject areas, and by maintaining a policing practice to insure that auxiliary personnel are not employed to undertake professional responsibilities.

The state department of education should establish machinery for devising guidelines for school districts and for setting up reasonable proficiency requirements. All professional education associations should be and should remain informed on the issues involved in selection, training and assignment of auxiliary personnel.

The local education association should be aware of the functions defined for aides and insure that those functions are being fulfilled properly. The association should also assume the responsibility of informing the community of teacher aide practices.

Local educational associations can, with active participation, be the motivating force behind the new developments, the workshops for specific subjects or instructional techniques and should also work for school budget planning that will insure adequate supplies and equipment for every classroom.

An active and imaginative local educational association can participate in the selection and hiring of new school personnel as well as establish professional standards and continuing education requirements for its members. The association can campaign for and attain a sabbatical-leave program to allow professionals to travel and study. It could also create a fund to establish a scholar-in-residence program for the school system as well as publish pamphlets on topics of immediate concern to teachers and establish consultant and travel funds to enable and encourage professionals to participate and observe innovative classroom activities.

The pressures of our changing society have made the slow passive methods of the past obsolete. The teacher of today must be flexible and initiate changes to meet the challenge of today's turbulent world. We have reached the point where the motivation for this change is now identical with that of survival. [4]

How Does a School System Start a Teacher Aide Program?

The first step in initiating a teacher aide program is to obtain the school board's permission to investigate the educational aspects of such a program. Once the school board's permission has been obtained, the chief school administrator should assume the responsibility for carrying out an in-depth investigation.

While investigating this program, it should be taken into consideration that, whenever new roles appear within any organization, suspicion and apprehension increase which if not dismissed with true and reassuring facts will yield strong negative feelings.

Introduction of a teacher aide program is generally not an easy task for any system. Actually, many systems may be reluctant to give any support to the idea of employing subprofessionals because it is difficult to take a genuine interest in something that you know little about.

To take an active, interested role in the development and implementation of a teacher aide program, administrators and

---

[4] Patricia Ellis and Dorothy V. Meyer, "The Teacher Evaluates Innovations," *NEA Journal*, December, 1967.

teachers will need to recognize their ignorance in this area and take steps to acquire basic pertinent data which will yield meaningful, intelligent thinking.

The following article, published in "The Nation's Schools," in April 1964[5] gives eight basic hints on "Launching an Aide Program":

1. Select aides according to specific qualifications such as ability, desire to work with children, previous vocational training, and stature in the community.

2. Prepare aide job descriptions that spell out their specific duties and responsibilities.

3. Establish a clear understanding of the separation of the professional roles of teachers from those of aides, emphasizing that the teacher is in command under all classroom conditions.

4. Provide in-service or pre-service training.

5. Orient aides in the school philosophy, practices and their place in the community.

6. Designate someone, such as the principal, to have general charge of all aides in his school.

7. Strive to make hiring of aides a cooperative undertaking between administration and teachers.

8. Evaluate the program at regular intervals.

Once an aide program has been initiated, an advisory committee of school administrators, supervisors, teachers, aides,

---

[5] Marilyn H. Cutler, "Teacher Aides Are Worth the Effort," *Nation's Schools*, April, 1964, p. 67-69, p. 116-118.

parents, community leaders and university consultants should be established. This committee should serve an evaluative function and suggest improvements in the utilization of aides. This may seem redundant and time-consuming, but if a teacher aide program is to be successful, it should have a continuous advisory committee to eliminate questions concerning the merits of the educational program by constantly updating the program to keep it effective.

What Can School Boards of Education do to Help Initiate and Maintain a Teacher Aide Program?

School boards of education can help initiate a teacher aide program by giving the concept formal recognition and sanction. The second phase would be for the local school board to have the chief school administrator investigate all phases of the teacher aide program and determine the most feasible and proper course of action to follow for their particular educational system.

If after basic research and investigation the board still favors the employment of a teacher aide program, they should then delegate to the school administration the power to pursue and set up a structured aide program in accordance with their decisions.

When choosing a particular plan for implementation of the teacher aide program the goals of the program must be clearly stated, legally sanctioned and implemented by precisely organized procedures. Organization of the program should include disciplinary action, explanation of responsibilities, salary schedules and fringe benefits and possibilities for upward mobility.

If the teacher aide program is to ever become an integral part of any educational program, it is essential that the involved local boards of education give it status through recognition and support. Regardless of how innovative a teacher aide program may be it will be doomed to failure if it is treated as a temporary adjunct, or dangling appendage to educational systems.

Must All Levels of Leadership be Totally Committed to the Teacher Aide Concept for it to be Successful?

No, it is not necessary, but it would be easier to initiate and maintain a teacher aide program under such ideal circumstances.

For the program to be initiated it must be approved by the board of education because the board of education controls budgetary allowances and gives legal sanction to all functions and activities within the school system.

If a principal does not want to have a teacher aide program in his particular school, the board of education can force him to accept it. However, the program will be more successful if the principal approves and encourages its implementation.

Some Teachers may not want to accept an aide and should not be forced to accept one for many reasons. Many teachers want and will actively seek the assistance of an aide. We can hope that the enthusiasm will be contagious as reluctant teachers see the program in action and the benefits resulting from it.

What Role Should Local School Administrators Take in Initiating a Teacher Aide Program?

By definition of his position, the local school administrator should take a major, active role in initiating the teacher aide program in his school system.

The local school administrator should:

1. Invite protagonistic and antagonistic teacher aide speakers to an open discussion to help in answering the questions on the teacher aide program.

2. Inform the school board of the benefits and pitfalls of a teacher aide program.

3. Seek and encourage school board approval.

4. Meet with local education associations to discuss the concept, develop an ideology and plan a course of action.

5. Seek and encourage the approval and support of the local educational association.

6. Meet with the faculty and explain the rationale for and the administrator's interest in the teacher aide program.

7. Appoint a committee of interested faculty members to conduct an in-depth study on the employment of teacher aides, to be presented to all concerned and necessarily involved individuals.

8. Keep parents, civic organizations and residents of the community informed on the action involved in teacher aide employment and deployment.

It is the duty of the local school administrators to present an analysis of the teacher aide concept and a proposed program with their views on its local application in a true and unbiased manner.

One of the most important steps in promoting the acceptance of a teacher aide program is to give proof that the foundations for operation have been firmly established. This will assure all persons involved that the program is well-developed, well-structured and well-disciplined.

Once the deployment guidelines have been founded, it is imperative that the program be presented to and receive the approval of the board of education, the administrative staff, the faculty, the non-teaching staff, the parents, the community and the students.

How Can Administrators, Faculty and Community Leaders Bring Parents into an Active Position in the Teacher Aide Program?

In the past, parents have suffered from a lack of status, communication skills, and information which has led to rigidity of opinion on both sides.

However, the teacher aide program is becoming the most natural and effective way of getting the parent out of the home and into the school and community by giving him an active role in the education of his children.

Parents from low-income areas have been and are faced with a two-sided disadvantage on the home front. Often those who take positions of leadership are rejected by their peers and sometimes the new leaders assume the middle class values and reject their own people.

To overcome this two-phased problem the administrators and faculty must select parents to serve as aides while stressing the educational goals. School-community advisory boards with as many parents as feasibly possible should be established to represent all viewpoints and to work together toward a realistic analysis of the program and its implementation with emphasis on maximization of the contributions of both groups toward quality education. If the number of active parents is increased it is likely that the wall between the active parent and the parent who is afraid or feels too inadequate to be active will fade.

What Can the Parents and Interested Citizenry do to Help Their Teacher Aide Program Get Started?

Parents and interested citizenry should first become informed about the issues and problems as well as advantages involved in the implementation of auxiliary personnel. They should visit other schools in which aides are employed to see aides in action in order to better understand the working function of an aide.

Once informed, parents can encourage school board members, administrators and teachers to partake in discussion groups concerned with the manner in which auxiliary personnel can assist with the vital job of education. If a genuine effort is made to bring information to the administrators and faculty, there will be a more genuine interest and effort on their part.

The school board should be requested to study the teacher aide concept in depth and its implementation in accordance with their school system. They should then present an unbiased report concerning the feasibility and advisability of such a program for their particular district. The report should be distributed to all potentially involved personnel and interested parents and citizenry.

Only if parents and interested citizenry take an informed, active interest in the program can they effectively induce a reluctant school board to pursue the teacher aide concept. A belligerent demand is not as likely to initiate effective action as will a sincere, informed request.

How Can the Parent Teacher Associations (PTA) Help Initiate and Sustain a Teacher Aide Program?

Across the nation there are more than 47,000 local units of the PTA, each with a vested interest in making this a better world for the children and youth of the country. Since its inception in 1897, the members of the PTA have represented a true cross section of democratic America. The members of the organization, whether businessman or farmer, homemaker or professional have a common purpose: promoting the well-being of children and youth in the community, the school and the home.

The overriding principle of the PTA is to assure that children will have the most favorable climate in which to achieve their fullest potential. The PTA is charged with the responsibility of:

Insuring the quality of educational standards
Improving the quality of school facilities

Enhancing education for all children and youth

Encouraging close relations between parents and teachers

Building closer cooperation between the school administrators and the community

Encouraging individual members to be informed and take an active part in building better educational programs

Giving guidance to parents and encouraging them in dealing with parent-student-teacher problems.

The success of a teacher aide program is largely dependent upon the support it receives from parents and members of the local community. Local PTA's can keep their members informed on key educational issues and research findings through the national and local PTA publications and thereby encourage a ready acceptance of the teacher aide program.

Today's PTA has set as its goal the education of every child to his fullest potential. To reach this goal the PTA must be willing to work for better educational programs and schools. It has been evidenced that, in fact, the PTA can be one of the greatest sources of teacher aides if the local unit takes an active part in the initiation and maintenance of the teacher aide program.

If the PTA is to take an active part in the initiation and maintenance of the teacher aide program it must take an active role in the planning and development of all phases of the teacher aide program. There must be an amicable relationship between parent-teacher-administrator to enable ready acceptance and approval of the teacher aide program.

How Can the Community be Convinced of the Need and Value of a Teacher Aide Program?

When seeking implementation of and funds for a teacher aide program, professionals will probably be asked: "Why does a teacher need help in the classroom?" and "Why do we have to spend additional tax dollars to support someone doing a job that the teacher is paid to do?" [6]

Obviously the professional knows what his needs are and what his limits are and it is he who can best determine if additional help in the classroom is needed. But, unless the community is well informed, its members will be alienated toward the teacher aide program and offer little support if not direct opposition.

To avoid this problem, parents must be made to feel as if they are a part of the educational process. There should be parent participation on steering committees and discussion groups. Every effort should be made to inform and involve as many citizens as possible by PTA and civic group discussions, direct and extensive coverage by local newspapers of plans and decisions concerning the program, followed by detailed reports of the program in progress.

Information brings involvement which yields cooperation.

How Should the Teacher Aide Program Idea be Introduced to the Teaching Staff?

The question that should be asked of today's teachers should not be whether they wish to see changes implemented such as the teacher aide program but whether or not they want to have a part in establishing and guiding its depth and direction.

The whole concept of education is rapidly changing, but as in any structured function, it is difficult to break away from traditional practices. There is an inherent fear of the far-reaching

---

[6] Clarence Lacny, Utilizing Teacher Aides in the Jackson, Michigan Public Schools, "A Dual Opportunity," Jackson Public Schools, 1970.

effects of an educational mistake that causes educators to be more reluctant to change tried and trusted practices for new concepts.

The demands of contemporary living have increased, causing the vast expansion of school curricula. The diversification of methodology and instructional techniques and a greater range of and demand for services has in reality made the idea of a teacher's job as strictly teaching unrealistic.

The demands from all social forces on today's teacher are greater than they have ever been at any other time in the history of mankind. Our specializing society can no longer afford to tolerate over-extended generalists. This demands that educators experiment and investigate new avenues of staff utilization.

Teachers must become active advocates of changes that have the potential to enhance education. Differentiated roles for teaching personnel must always be viewed and weighed in reference to the value it has for the student recipient.

One of the best ways to introduce the idea of teacher aide employment to the professional is through the local educational association by the school administrator. Once the idea of implementation of the teacher aide concept has been announced and the employment and deployment practices have been explained, the administrator should open the program to discussion, consideration and investigation by members of the association.

Administrators should realize that the introduction of a teacher aide program into most school systems will not meet with immediate blanket approval. To gain the majority vote of approval of the local education association, many questions must first be resolved.

One question that will inevitably be raised is, "What is the aide's position in relation to the faculty and the administrative staff?"

Another is, "From what sources will the money come to pay for the aides?"

Once these basic questions have been satisfactorily answered the administrator should then explain why an aide program is being considered. Traditionally, the primary goal of the school has been to generate academic achievement on the part of the student. The administrator should emphasize the fact that, in order for students to receive first-rate education, their teachers must be provided with opportunities to maintain first-rate standards.

Everything that a teacher aide will do will be done in the direction of assisting a teacher. In order for a teacher aide program to be effective, there must be a positive relationship between the teacher and the aide at every level.

Considering this factor, one of the most appropriate methods of introducing teacher aides into the school system may be to ask teachers to volunteer to accept teacher aides on a trial basis. The first year of operation of the program will be crucial. Its success will be based upon and judged by recruitment, training, assignment, and the degree to which the latent reluctance to change has been overcome.

For those considering initiating the program the words of Francis Bacon may provide impetus:

> "He who will not try new remedies must expect new evils, for time is the greatest innovator."

What Can Local Faculties do to Initiate a Teacher Aide Program?

Through its local education association, the faculty can become a strong motivating force behind the development of a teacher aide program. Faculty members interested in initiating a teacher aid program should first study the feasibility of adopting such a program in their particular system. For any teacher aide program to meet with success it must have the good will and support of the faculty and staff members involved. To achieve realistic success, the teachers involved must believe and be self-convinced of the value of the teacher aide program.

Initially a study should be made of the procedures and policies involved in operating such a nonprofessional program. With this in mind, the goals should be carefully weighed.

A faculty committee should visit several school systems presently employing aides, noting the duties which the aides are assigned. They should be free in questioning students, aides, teachers and administrators. Reaction, both pro and con, should be accurately recorded. People who have had an experience with a teacher aide program are an extremely vital source of information and should not be ignored.

The faculty committee should then determine and define the nonprofessional program which they would like to initiate in their school system. The study should then be presented to the local education association for approval. If approved by the local education association, it should then be presented to the local school board for action and implementation. If the program receives administrative approval and is implemented, the faculty should vigorously support the aide program.

What Can Community Colleges do to Help Teacher Aide Programs Get Started in Their Communities?

Community Colleges can first survey the community to determine if there is a need for a teacher aide training program in the community. A survey is necessary to enable practical and realistic planning. Planning without the foundation of an accurate survey often is a waste of time, money and energy. To be of service, planning must be done with a realistic background of the needs of the community and the challenges posed by these needs.

If a teacher aide program is being considered or is in the developmental stages in the local community, the community college can determine which types of aides would be most appropriate for the community. When this has been determined, the community college could develop a training program for aides of the type or types which the community college research group feels would best fit the needs of the community. By developing teacher aide training programs, community colleges could take the lead in initiating proper teacher aide programs in the community.

The community college could then set up an in-plant - in-service training program to meet the needs of the community and the teacher aide program. Because of the location of the community college within the community, the college can easily keep vigil over the program and alter the training program to meet the changing needs of the community.

In meeting community needs the community college could develop a teacher aide training program as a part of a continuing education training program for local citizens. In this manner adults as well as pupils would benefit from the teacher aide program.

What Can Colleges do to Help Initiate Teacher Aide Programs?

Colleges and universities can begin teacher aide programs with the aim of preparing teachers to train their auxiliary personnel. Senior colleges and universities can plan and prepare to give educational guidance to junior colleges and school districts and give ancillary services to their professional educators.

They might also consider development of a plan in which prospective teachers would spend a semester or a year in a paid-aide capacity in addition to the student teaching or internship which is a standard of professional preparation.

Development of the program for direct training of auxiliary personnel might incorporate educational opportunities for auxiliaries who desire to qualify for advancement to the professional level. It might also incorporate the expanded role-concept of the teacher as one who organizes resources, both human and material, in meeting the needs of the students.

Most aides will benefit from additional in-service training and support after they begin working in schools. Informal seminars and assistance of resource personnel may be all that is necessary to keep aides abreast of new developments and methods which are pertinent to the aide's work.

The aide position should be viewed as a desirable, satisfying, status-giving terminal occupation for those who have no desire to acquire further education. However, opportunities for promising personnel who have the desire to realize their potential must be created and remain available. In the colleges and universities, programs could be developed which would give college credit for aide training and classroom experiences, if the aide so desired.

Educational institutions have continually viewed adult out-of-school upgrading and training programs as a function of either government or industry. Presently, jobs must be created at the rate of 25,000 per week to maintain our present rate of employment. While realizing that scientific progress phases out far more unskilled jobs than skilled jobs, one must realize that the same science creates jobs. With these thoughts in mind, educators must bring new hope and encouragement to those taking steps forward toward a new career.

Charles Keller said, "Education must be flexible and experimental yet quality centered and academically sound." With this in mind, a system could eventually be set up which would allow aides to gain further education along lines similar to those of various nursing programs such as training for state licensing. Another possibility is developing an auxiliary personnel program that would encourage and assist aides in becoming full-fledged teachers.

Pitfalls in Initiating and Administering a Teacher Aide Program: What are They and How Can They be Avoided?

In implementing and administering a teacher aide program many pitfalls and drawbacks will be encountered; however, they are not insurmountable.

There will always be the problem of the over-zealous aide who becomes officious and takes liberties and assumes authorities to which she is not entitled. However, the well-informed aide knows her limitations and will go no farther than the teacher will permit her to go.

Initially, teacher aides may have difficulty in working efficiently with the students and the teacher. The aide may find it difficult to gain an understanding of her role and attain the students' acceptance.

The aide's apprehension at the time of initial employment is to be expected. Aides may be extremely conscious of the difference in their backgrounds, behavior and patterns of speech apart from those prevailing in the school. They may become defensive of the unknown expectations of the strange area and activities. Training without actual employment tends to provoke anxiety and leads to frustration, since even the most sincere assurance of employment sometimes proves impossible to implement.

Training has been identified as the essential factor in the effective use of auxiliary personnel. To avoid creating a gap between the pre-service and the in-service program for aides, parallel programs of training and work might be ideal. Joint responsibility of the schools and colleges in planning, financing and staffing the program is essential. If possible, hiring should precede training to enable trainees to be given orientation for actual job assignment. Employment without training appears to present many problems.

The teacher is the pivotal person in the teacher-teacher aide relationship. She is responsible and accountable for the teaching in the classroom and the utilization of the aide. However, the teacher must be secure in her position and socialized so as to view her aide as an assistant rather than a threat.

The aide is an employee of the classroom teacher, hence the teacher should be involved in the interviewing and hiring of her teacher aide.

Some teachers will argue that they cannot teach effectively with an aide in the classroom. Others say that a teacher aide will cause more work than they are worth. Teachers may argue that poor salaries may make it difficult to keep good aides, while parents may argue that the students will have less personal contact. Uninformed parents and the community may protest the employment and additional cost of nonprofessional help.

To combat these judgments predicated on ignorance, provide extensive material with facts and figures on the benefits of a teacher aide program such as the articles "To What Extent Can Teacher Aides Free the Teacher's Time to Teach?" and "What Benefits Have Resulted From the Teacher Aide Program?" which are included in this presentation.

Most aides are seeking a new direction or a change in their lives. Employment with opportunity for upward mobility is essential to a successful program. There should be an opportunity for upward mobility but it should not be compulsory.

The institutionalization of auxiliary help within the school system is still a hope and a dream. To give it permanence it must first be resolved in the minds of the teachers, teacher aides, and the community that the teacher aides are not trained for temporary uncertain "dead end" jobs but for stable open-ended employment.

CHAPTER VI

ENHANCING THE TEACHER AIDE PROGRAM

It is the teachers, and especially those who deal with the very young, who have made the character and conscience of America what it is today. It is they who will continue to implant ethics, decency, character and a determination to do the very best. They have made America what it is and must continue to be.

Bernard   Baruch

All the high hopes which I entertain for a more glorious future for the human race are built upon the elevation of the teacher's profession and the enlargement of the teacher's usefulness.

Horace Mann

Enhancing the Teacher Aide Program

Can a Teacher Aide Program Enhance and Stimulate an Entire School System?

An evaluative committee has agreed that teacher aide programs tend to stimulate educational services in two ways. First, assuming normal professional competence on the part of the professional teacher, the aide program insures a better administered classroom with all necessary routines carefully monitored. Secondly, the aide program creates a demand for more services, such as instructional aides, by underscoring any deficiencies that may exist.[1]

The employment of teacher aides will stimulate the use of audio-visual aides to the point where it exceeds the per-pupil use of instructional material of non-aided classrooms.

---

[1] A Revision of a Cooperative Study for the Better Utilization of Teacher Competencies, Final Evaluation Report, an Evaluation Report Prepared by an Outside Evaluating Committee, Central Michigan University, Mt. Pleasant, Michigan, 1958.

To the point that teacher aides will increase the demands for instructional services by uncovering deficiencies, the program will also increase the demands for educational expenditures.

A properly structured aide program offers an efficiently effective method of utilizing intelligent and highly competent individuals in an educational situation despite the fact that the aides may not have had professional teacher training.

Professional educators alone are not sufficient to insure academic success with all students. Aides can give teachers realistic knowledge of a community and assist a teacher in active involvement in the community which will bring the teacher a step closer to her students in bridging the communications gap.

What Can and Must the State Department of Education do to Enhance Teacher Aide Programs?

Each state must individually study the teacher aide issue and then solidly determine its position regarding aide certification. If teacher aide programs are to become a valid and reliable educational entity, within a state, the state must provide it with legality and recognition.

The state departments of education must, either individually or collectively, set the certification codes with an outline of basic requirements and guidelines of duties for each type of aide given certification. It would also be desirable to have the state set the basic guidelines for the use and training of locally sanctioned aide programs.

How has the Federal Government Encouraged Teacher Aide Programs?

The Elementary and Secondary Education Act of 1965 provided many school districts with funds for employment of teacher aides to assist with programs designed to help culturally deprived children. In 1965 the U. S. Office of Education provided written guidelines [2] which suggested use of sub-professional personnel in assisting teachers in educating culturally deprived students.

The guidelines emphasize two basic reasons for hiring indigenous parents: (1) It will provide a vital and realistic service to the school, teachers, students, community and parents, and (2) it will serve as positive effort in bridging the communication gap between home and school.

Title I has seriously challenged traditional educational practices by introducing techniques that promise to benefit middle and upper class children as well. Title I has allowed local administrators to explore varying community resources. The use of paid and volunteer aides indigenous to the community serves to strengthen school-community ties. This approach has given parents a fresh desire to improve and to advance their own education which in turn yields a better self-concept. These factors combined have caused many parents to leave the welfare role and to become self-supporting, multi-contributing members of society.

Teacher aide programs furnish disadvantaged communities and individuals with improved and new career opportunities.

Parents from all walks of life want to help their children succeed, especially in school. However, many do not know how, have the time, or the personal belief that they can help their children in school. Past conditioning has made the schools enemy territory to many segments of our population. Unsound educational concepts and attitudes are rapidly dissipating and school

---

[2] *Guidelines for Special Programs for Educationally Deprived Children*, Department of Health, Education and Welfare, Office of Education, Draft, October 5, 1965, p. 20.

administrators are welcoming and involving all community seg-ments. School communities are not only listening to pleas to get involved and to try and resolve varying community problems but are also demanding that certain changes be undertaken.

Educational research continually indicates that parents in many areas feel isolated or ignored by their local schools. In order to combat this Title I, ESEA, has established the criteria that cause parents to have a larger voice in determining the educational programs and services to be provided their children. Basically, this new criteria gives emphasis to the organization of formal advisory committees. One chief function of local advisory committees is to help resolve conflicting interests.

Title I preschool programs emphasize language development and readiness activities, with health, nutrition, psychological, and social work services being provided. Parental involvement is stressed through home-school visits, parent education classes, field trips, conferences, with the employment of parents as either paid or volunteer being emphasized.

In 1967 the Education Professions Bill [3] made it possible for state education agencies to submit state plans which would include programs utilizing teacher aides. These plans would also provide pre-service and in-service training designed to enable aides to better perform their duties. This act forces state educational agencies to move on the use of teacher aides if the state receives federal funds.

In order for a state to participate in this program, it must designate the programs to be used and show developmental

---

[3] Education Profession Act, P.L. 90-35 Sec. 520, Title V, Part B., Higher Education Act of 1965, amended.

plans for both long and short range policies and procedures for the use of federal funds to obtain and train teacher aides. [4]

Should Teacher Aides be Admitted to Teaching Staff Meetings?

To a high degree, either a positive or negative response to the question depends upon the rank and status of the teacher aide in the school and the individual classroom in which she is employed.

If a teacher aide is not part of the teacher-teacher aide team concept but solely a teacher aide, the teacher may resent an infringement upon her professional territory. Aides should not be invited to attend teaching staff meetings at the risk of alienating the professional teachers.

In the case where a teacher-teacher aide team exists, both teacher and aide would benefit from the aide's presence at teaching staff meetings.

Information is best obtained firsthand. Teachers are human beings, and information which they give to their aides may be garbled with personal bias or the teacher may simply omit information of which she does not approve.

In a meeting closed to aides, the pool of ideas is reduced. If an aide does volunteer an idea to her supervising teacher, the teacher may be reluctant to submit it in an open meeting.

Many ideas are shaped in teaching staff meetings on the basis of classroom experiences. Because teacher aides also have this

---

[4] *Guide for Preparing a State Plan for Attracting and Qualifying Teachers to Meet Critical Teacher Shortages*, Part B, subpart 2, of the Education Professions Development Act (Title V of the Higher Education Act of 1965).

classroom experience, they should be allowed to watch the formation of new ideas and, upon invitation of the staff, take an active, contributive part in teaching staff meetings.

Should Teacher Aides Have a Voice in Educational Policy-Making?

When faced with this question in a state-wide survey, taken in the State of Michigan, of 2,992 teachers and administrators, a scant 458 were in favor of allowing teacher aides a voice in educational policy-making, while 2,196 were opposed and 338 expressed no opinion.

As to the question of whether or not teacher aides should be admitted to teaching staff meetings, 1,760 were in favor while 1,042 were opposed and 190 expressed no opinion.

Concerning supervision of teacher aides, there was an overwhelming teacher vote of 1,974 for teacher supervision of aides, 1,062 favored supervision by administrators and 624 favored specific teacher aide supervisors.

If schools dedicate themselves to the conceptual philosophy that every child is to receive a first-rate educational experience, our schools must be willing to listen with an attentive ear to all voices. Educators must realize that having a voice and an opportunity to speak, is not in itself a mandate for action.

Administrators must encourage and inculcate new approaches to staff and curricular development whenever possible.

Innovation and dynamism in a meaningful learning system will only be found where the professional educators view themselves as learners along with their nonprofessionals and students. Any voice that can offer new awareness or prospects of a new dimension to any topic or problem should be encouraged.

Most contemporary teachers are unenlightened in reference to concepts dealing with employment and deployment of teacher aides. Primarily, this is a result of two forces: 1) teachers have been conditioned to the belief that teachers are and should be the sole innovators and expediters of all things relating to the teaching and well-being of students entrusted to their care, and 2) teacher training institutions have failed to present the teacher aide concept in a realistic and meaningful manner.

Teachers must be prepared to face the new demands which are constantly facing the teaching profession. Teachers must dare to leave the tried and tested to try the new ideas which can help teachers to become more efficient and proficient in their specialties.

Two new concepts which bring added demands to the teacher are the idea that student development is increased and improved with additional adult control and that idea which stresses preventive educational measures rather than relying on remedial education.

The two concepts, when applied, will bring teacher aides into the classroom to better meet the needs of the students. The teachers must be prepared to meet the entrance of the new person with new ideas.

Should the Same Professional Teaching Membership be Tendered to Teacher Aides?

A survey of 2,992 teachers and administrators taken in 1968 in the State of Michigan, by this author, indicated that 309 were in favor of professional teaching membership, 2,407 were opposed, and 276 abstained.

In regard to a semi-professional membership for teacher aides, 1,867 were in favor of such a membership, 718 were opposed and 149 abstained.

The idea of organizing or belonging is an inherent quality in all groups bound by even a remote commonality. With this in mind the question is where do teacher aides best fit into the educational system—at the nonprofessional, semi-professional or professional level?

Early resolution of this question would eliminate many meetings and prevent much friction in personality clashes.

Teachers should view teacher aides as their assistants and identify with their problems. The degree of identity formulated by the teacher to her aide will determine the amount of concern for their problems. It should be understood that teachers who over-identify do their aides at least as great a disservice as those who under-identify with their aides.

Contemporary educational thought favors a semi-professional organization for teacher aides. However, current administrators feel that teacher aides should either be classified nonprofessional or professional. They feel that two bargaining units are enough to placate each without the creation of a third. Actually, many would like to see teacher aides remain strictly an hourly salaried group working on a contractual basis without any tangible connection to the schools over and above the hourly wage rate.

The current trend toward rapid implementation of teacher aides in the classrooms yields programs ranging from the informal, nondescriptive to the formal, highly-structured. However, investigation indicates that semi-professional or associate memberships are being offered to teacher aides who have been required to undergo at least one year of post-high school training.

In time this will probably be lowered. Those who have less than one year of post high school training will probably remain in a non-teaching union arrangement. This type of system of determining salaries would also serve as an inducement for those wishing to upgrade themselves.

The need for teacher aides to identify and belong is a crucial factor that must be dealt with now. Teacher aides are here and are here to stay until something better replaces them. Proper planning is needed. The sooner and more effectively these basic problems are resolved the better will be the transition to and operation of the teacher aide program.

Should a Special Semi-Professional Membership be Created to Cover Aides?

Status of the aide in regard to employment and bargaining procedures is not yet clearly defined. However, as organized teacher-aide programs are developed and implemented, the employment group will begin to assume a separate structure unless it is incorporated into another existing unit which exists solely as a bargaining agency in the employment structure with special emphasis on wages and fringe benefits. Membership in such a unit is imminent for it is idealistic to believe that such a group would provide services for the teacher aide group without assessment of fees.

Because the employment group is sub-professional, as it organizes it will be clearly identified with definite lines of distinctions from professional and nonprofessional groups. Administrators should be prepared to face this division which could yield the development of a third bargaining unit.

The quick rise of the third force should be expected because of the organized educational training and the distinction between professional and nonprofessional employment groups will give members of the group specific needs and interests which must be tended to.

If administrators desire to subdue plans for a third and separate bargaining unit, they should initiate plans for incorporating the aide employment group into the professional bargaining unit or the nonprofessional bargaining unit. This would give the aide employment unit the status it needs as well as a means for handling intra-unit interests and a formal organized structure for extra-unit interests.

What Factors Appear to Enhance the Condition of Learning for Teacher Aides?

Factors that appeared to enhance and to facilitate learning as viewed, investigated and identified by visitation teams and 15 individual demonstration project directors are:

1. Cooperative planning by school systems, institutions of higher learning, community action agencies, professional associations, instructional staff, and participants.

2. Skill training which is realistic in terms of local employment opportunities, but also geared to future potentialities in the utilization of auxiliary personnel by the local school system.

3. Inclusion of both auxiliaries and teachers in the trainee group, preferably as teams from a given school — teams that will work together in an actual school situation after the training.

4. Opportunity for experiential learning coupled with scheduled time for daily analysis of their practicum experiences by the teacher-auxiliary teams, and shared planning for the next class situation based on this analysis.

5. Theoretical instruction for auxiliaries in foundations of child development, interpersonal relations, the life conditions of disadvantaged pupils, and the school as an institution.

6. Basic education for auxiliaries in communication and language arts leading to high school equivalency where necessary, as well as skill training in technical and service operations such as typing, record keeping, and operation of audio-visual equipment.

7. Availability of individual and/or group counseling to help participants deal with their own personal needs,

as well as their growth in job performance, to foster interaction among professionals and nonprofessionals, and to help teachers accept their new role as orchestrator of other adults in the classroom. [5]

[5] Garda W. Bowman and Gordon J. Klopf, "New Careers and Roles in the American School" A study conducted for the Office of Economic Opportunity, New York: Bank Street College of Education, September 1967, p. 36-37, p. 153-154.

CHAPTER VII

CLASSIFICATION OF TEACHER AIDES: THE BRIGHTON CONCEPT

Since the school is the one institution set up for strictly educative purposes, one would justifiably expect it to provide for children a richer and more varied and stimulating environment than exists anywhere else in the community.

John A. Hockett and E. W. Jacobson, *Modern Practices in the Elementary School*, ed., Boston, Ginn, 1943, p. 125.

Classification of Teacher Aides: The Brighton Concept

Is it Necessary for Each Aide Program to Have a
Definite Individual Structure, Function, and Purpose?

Yes . . . . . it is imperative that each type aide program perform only the function for which it has been given structure and authority. Initial planning should take into account factors peculiar to each district and decide which type aide program or programs best fit into each individual school district and that best meets its particular needs.

In so doing, each aide category should be viewed with a pro and con discussion. Once the type aide program or programs are decided upon, it is necessary to take into consideration specific plans for financing, staffing, training, assigning, supervising, implementing, researching, follow-up and evaluation as part of the total undertaking.

For the implementation of any aide program, it is necessary for the program to first be conceived and studied, then made operable and answerable to a structured overall master aide employment-deployment plan. Proper planning is important for it will aide insurance of the program's success and allow it a safer implementation for entry, faster, sounder progress and make it more conducive to progress measurement. Each aide employed in a school system, whether that of a sporadically used volunteer or that of a full-time paid staff member, should operate only within a planned and enforced categorical structure.

How Many Different Teacher Aide Classifications Should There be? THE BRIGHTON CONCEPT

There should be eight different and distinct Teacher Aide classifications:

Student Aides
Mother Aides
Father Aides
Volunteer Aides
Special Aides
Practical Aides
Certified Aides
Reader and Grader Aides

The above aide classification categories are almost self-explanatory. Each aide category performs specific functions, within a structural framework. No school would need or be expected to use all eight types of aides described, but there is no reason why they could not if they so desired.

If the teacher aide concept is ever to become a meaningful on-going and vital part of education, it must have order. For a program to have order it needs to possess a descriptive and communicative structure. Any aide program that does not provide a descriptive and communicative structure is at best a temporary stopgap operation subject to basic whims and prejudices for direction.

Who Should Determine the Classification of Aides?

The classification of aides should either be based on a certification system or a sanctioning system. Basic requirements of each aide classification should be defined by the State Department of Education or its equivalent in each state.

Certification and sanctioning codes should be readily available to all interested school personnel. The primary responsibility for the employment and proper deployment of teacher aides should remain with the head educational administrator (Superintendent).

Superintendents could then delegate authority to sub-administrators or to the local educational association for implementation and operation of the aide program. The local educational association should be given a strong consultive, if not active, administrative role in the employment and deployment of teacher aides.

Who Should Give Certification or Sanction to Teacher Aides?

Certification means giving license to sanctioned practices upon completion of defined requirements by a state's top-ranking legally constituted educational authority. All teacher aides do not need to be certified, many can be locally sanctioned. However, all aides engaged in advanced educational deployment practices should be certified.

Certification for advanced teacher aides should come only from the State Department of Education. All training institutions engaged in preparing advanced teacher aides should be approved only by the State Department of Education upon the meeting of required standards. The aide training institutions would be the recommending institution for certification.

119

Sanctioning means giving credence to a practice after certain criteria have been met. Teacher aide programs which are menial and clerical in nature should not require state certification, only local sanction. All training, employment and deployment of these teacher aide categories should primarily be the responsibility of the local administrator and policed by the local education association.

What are Student Aides?

The student aide classification would include *any elementary* or *secondary* student who is used in either a paid or voluntary capacity to help teachers in any of their duties either within or without the school.

What Type and How Much In-Service Training Should Student Aides Have?

Interested students should first attend an introductory meeting describing, in detail, the functions of a student aide program. All student aides should be recruited, trained, assigned and guided by an officially sanctioned and designated organization within the school system. A Future Teachers Club under the sponsorship and guidance of the local education association would be one means of attending to many perfunctory duties.

Those accepted into the student aide program would be trained basically in four phases: 1) an introductory session, 2) an indoctrination session, 3) periodic teacher aide consultations and planning sessions, 4) group or club sessions.

The number of teacher aide consultations and planning sessions along with club or group sessions would be varied depending upon organizational structure, need, and personalities involved.

What Type of Duties Could Student Aides Perform?

Duties that student aides could perform are:

1. Maintain students' weight and measurement charts.

2. Help conduct students to varying school activities.

3. Display student's work.

4. Write lessons and instructions on blackboards.

5. Write out daily schedule on blackboard.

6. Care for a small group while the teacher is busy with the majority of the class in another activity.

7. Keep library records, keep records of books read and projects completed by students.

8. Supervise or referee educational and recreational games.

9. Serve as a class reader and storyteller.

10. Conduct individual students to appointments within the school building.

11. Serve as a host or hostess at Parent-Teacher conferences.

12. Help a child develop motor coordination.

13. Help individual children identify and form letters and numbers.

14. Make name tags for students, etc.

15. Duplicate instructional materials.

16. Prepare stencils for drill materials.

17. File instructional material for teacher.

18. Make Visual Aids.

19. Gather supplemental books and materials for teacher and class.

20. Serve as an oral reading listener.

21. Distribute and collect specific lesson material.

22. Prepare, set up, operate, and return instructional materials and equipment.

23. Prepare materials for art, science, and special projects.

24. Construct various charts.

25. Aid with special educational and home projects.

26. Check to see that students are correctly following teachers' directions.

27. Maintain representative work folders for each student.

28. Help students in lunchroom.

29. Assist with recess and noon home duties.

30. Run errands for the teacher.

31. Decorate the classroom.

32. Arrange bulletin board and keep it current.

33. Collect milk, lunch, movie, picture, and other minor monies.

34. Assist teacher on field trips.

35. Check pupils for weather dress and aid with dressing difficulties.

36. Serve as hall monitors.

37. Patrol school buses.

38. Serve as a safety officer.

39. Check out recreational and special equipment.

40. Serve as an intersection crossing guard.

41. Help slow children with letter, number and word identification.

42. Assist a child with color identification.

43. Assist teacher with preparation and serving of food.

44. Assist in physical needs of the children, such as going to the washroom and washing up, etc.

45. Write for free and inexpensive materials.

46. Help take care of classroom pets and plants.

47. Free teacher from unnecessary classroom interruptions.

48. Help provide greater safety supervision for students.

49. File and catalogue material.

50. Play piano, etc.

51. Help students locate materials.

52. Move among students to see if work is being done correctly.

This list is not exclusive, nor is it meant to serve as a permissive guide or restrictive limit for every student aide program. The duties outlined give reference to the range and type of duties student aides could proficiently perform. It should be a teacher's prerogative to add or subtract basic housekeeping, bookkeeping, and storekeeping duties according to his view of the situational classroom needs. Montessorians have long utilized students to help other students learn in the classroom.

What are Mother Aides?

Mother aides are room mothers who volunteer to give a certain amount of their time to assist in various classroom connected activities. Mother aides are often called room mothers. Their involvement is generally one in which short amounts of time blocks are promised and later expended in preparation and carrying out various, sporadically spaced classroom functions.

What Type and How Much In-Service Training Should Mother Aides Have?

Mother aides should be required to attend at least one indoctrination session. The indoctrination session should highlight the needs, responsibilities and role of their new duties.

The follow-up session should be planned to follow through on the indoctrination session and bring out other points needing clarification. The indoctrination and follow-up sessions should do more than acquaint the mother aides with their new duties and responsibilities. It should give them greater exposure and bring about new awarenesses of the complex educational system.

The deployment of mother aides would for the most part be confined to one basic classroom, generally performing menial and perfunctory tasks.

What Duties Could be Performed by Mother Aides?

The mother aide classification does not take into account the factors of advanced training and special talents of mother aides. When outlining duties for the mother aide category, special talent and advanced training should be noted and integrated into the program, if the mother desires to work in that capacity. Mother aides should be utilized according to their capabilities and talents even though they may be in the mother aide category.

A mother aide should be able to perform all of the duties listed for student aides in addition to the following duties:

1. Supervise the loading and unloading of school buses.

2. Serve as a regular school bus driver.

3. Serve as a special school bus driver for field trips.

4. Conduct sick students either home or to a doctor.

5. Chaperone activities outside of school.

6. Supervise the lunchroom.

7. Supervise the halls during the noon hours.

8. Assist with student health care.

9. Supervise milk and lunch programs.

10. Plan and supervise indoor activities for inclement weather.

11. Manage the room library and keep it stocked with material from outside sources.

12. Inventory and account for non-consumable goods.

13. Serve as an adult confidant when needed.

14. Be available to students, as well as the teacher, when a "sounding board" or a "listening ear" is needed.

A mother aide program should be structured, scheduled, and consistent. Indiscriminate, sporadic and unstructured use of mother aides is unfair to the aide, the teacher, and especially to the students.

A mother aide program must be structured, scheduled and consistent if it is to play an integral part in the organized educational process.

What are Father Aides?

Father aides, like mother aides, are room fathers who volunteer to give certain amounts of their time to assist with various classroom connected activities.

The use of father aides will be a unique experience in many schools, for it will be the first step away from the tradition of matriarchal domination of teacher aides. Father aides may prove to be an answer to the lack of influence or exposure to adult masculinity in the schools as shown by contemporary research.

The father aide concept is based on the theory that both girls and boys benefit from the exposure to male patterning figures. Youth can develop a more wholesome role identification if exposed to more men in the learning situation.

Father aides need not be formally or highly trained. When selecting men for the position of father aides, emphasis should be placed on qualities of inspirational attitudes, imagination, creativity, friendly demeanor, patience, tolerance, ability to relate to children, an easily identifiable masculine attitude and above all, a sincere desire to work for and with children.

What Type and How Much In-Service Training Should Father Aides Have?

Room fathers or father aides should be required to attend a minimum of one indoctrination and one follow-up training session. The training sessions should be especially planned for this type of aide, clearly pointing out their specific duties and responsibilities.

What Duties Could be Performed by Father Aides?

In outlining duties for this aide category, the father aide classification does not take into consideration advanced training or special talents. If a father aide has advanced training or special talents and desires to work in that capacity, he should be dealt with accordingly, in the applicable aide category.

If necessary, a father aide should be able to perform all duties listed for student aides, in addition to those listed for mother aides. A well-structured father aide program could lead the way to new educational vistas for both students and teachers. The masculine influence has many possibilities if properly handled in a professional manner, in a well-organized program. The new and increased use of father aides in our schools is a relatively unexplored but challenging practice.

What are Volunteer Aides?

The volunteer aide program, as the name implies, is the offering of innumerable free services to schools by dedicated individuals. Therefore, the volunteer aide category must be open-ended in order to allow individuals of all capacities and availability status to volunteer their services.

This type aide program allows educational institutions to draw from a wide variety of unique abilities and talents which are found in every community.

Volunteer aides have a greater immediate need and deployment potential than any other aide category. However, the initial pre-planning and planned usage of volunteer aides will collectively require more time than any of the other aide programs.

What Type and How Much In-Service Training Should Volunteer Aides Have?

The type and amount of training desired for volunteer aides should be flexible and variable. The diversity of volunteer aide personnel in training and experience would often call for individualized in-service training.

The sophistication of in-service training would depend upon the aides' past experience and in their present planned deployment. Volunteer aides with special talents or unique abilities would probably be used by more than one teacher. Therefore, special scheduling and planning must be taken into account in order to insure proper utilization of the aide's time and ability.

A minimal in-service training program for volunteer aides should be at least two sessions: 1. indoctrination and 2. follow-up.

What are Volunteer Aides and What Duties Could They Perform?

Volunteer aides are men, women, and students, of all ages, from all walks of life, who are willing to give some of their time to help in the schools. They are bound by at least two factors of commonality: 1) they are interested and 2) they have the desire to help youth.

This type aide program, like all other aide categories, is designed to give teachers more time to teach and to create opportunities for time during which teachers can utilize their talents to greater advantage.

Extreme flexibility and adaptability are two requisites for a successful volunteer aide program. This personnel category has possibilities for a wide range of services.

Implementation of volunteer aides in schools can bring forth a multitude of new, enhancing educational and recreational insights. However, volunteer aides should perform only those duties which are in accordance with their qualifications and experience, as outlined under various aide categories.

This category was specifically designed for voluntary services; it was not intended to perform specific services.

In 1956 the Public Education Association of New York City initiated an experimental volunteer aide program to provide help for classroom teachers. The experiment enjoyed unusual success and in 1962 was formally incorporated into the school system. In 1964 the program found 640 volunteers giving 45,000 man-hours to the program.

This program is one of the best known volunteer aide programs. It was awarded a Ford Foundation grant in 1964, which gave promise to increasing the New York City program both in number and dimension. The grant also gave hope to the idea of national promotion of the volunteer aide concept. This program concentrated primarily on helping to provide enrichment programs for the gifted students and for those students with special needs.

Misgivings toward the volunteer program lie in the knowledge that it is a volunteer program. Some administrators believe that it is unfair to exploit the local citizenry, or find it difficult to make demands on and to administer a program that depends on non-employees.

The volunteer aide program as described above refers only to those connected with in-school or school-connected administration. Volunteer work has always been and will continue to be an American tradition.

Mass communication has created a keen awareness of social and educational inequities within our society. This awareness has caused concerned people with free time to volunteer portions of their time to serve and to help in their own best way to try and make the world a little better.

Many outside volunteer programs complementing and supplementing the academic effort of the school have met with success. Community organizations, churches, civic associations and clubs sponsor volunteer programs and often designate them as after-school or outside study centers.

Sources of volunteer aides are numerous and varied. Some cities find men and women of business and professional organizations providing needed educational enrichment in the schools on a continuous voluntary basis. One of the largest single sources of volunteer help is college and university students. (For further details of college volunteers see Appendix A.)

There is also a trend toward using volunteer assistants in team settings. The Reed Union School District (Belevedere-Tiburon-Corte Madera, California) has a new elementary building (Granada School) staffed by "volunteer instructional aides" in addition to various professional staff members and salaried team aides. The volunteers provide services equivalent to one and a half full-time workers for each team of about a hundred pupils. They help with library duties, the school health program (these are the "gray ladies"), and the instructional program. They assist the salaried aides by performing miscellaneous housekeeping functions, by providing receptionist and guide services for visitors, and by handling various clerical duties.

The team structure at the Granada School includes a highly experienced team leader, a team teacher (at the senior level) with average experience, a team teacher (at the junior level) who is a beginner, a salaried team intern, and one or two student teachers. Volunteers, however, are regarded as regular components of the staff. [1]

Partly because of the need in many schools for extra workers and partly because of a belief that school-home relationships

---

[1] Robert H. Anderson, *Teaching in a World of Change*, New York: Harcourt, Brace and World, 1966, Chapter 6, "The People Who Work With Teachers," p. 7.

are strengthened when parents play a role in the daily life of a school, it has long been a custom in certain school systems to use unpaid parent volunteers. These parents perform clerical functions, serve as library workers, help with cafeteria supervision, or assist the school nurse with health check-ups. Sometimes they provide actual teaching services such as tutoring. [2]

In order to meet the rising demands of volunteer groups in Chicago, the Human Relations Commission, an official agency of the city of Chicago, assumed the duties of leadership and direction for these groups. In 1965, after three years, there were more than 150 volunteer study centers giving help to students from pre-elementary to secondary grades, in addition to helping adults.

Outside volunteer work in education is finding readily receptive groups throughout the United States. Giving sanction to reliable outside volunteer aide programs where warranted and feasible has merit. However, they are not, even remotely, to be seen as an educational panacea. They are supplemental programs and must be viewed as such.

Volunteer programs of this nature are popular and easily initiated. Unfortunately, there are the ever-present dangers that these groups may become unjustly critical of the educational processes or inadvertently distract attention from the overall educational program need.

For a more comprehensive report on the benefits and pitfalls of volunteer aides in education, see: "Helping Hands," by Gayle Janowintz, [3] THE NATIONAL SCHOOL VOLUNTEER

---

[2] Ibid.

[3] Gayle Janowitz, *Helping Hands,* University of Chicago Press, Chicago, Illinois, 1965.

PROGRAM, which provides information on implementing volunteer programs,[4] or Appendix A.

What are Special Aides?

Special aides, as far as qualifications are concerned, could be classified in any of the aide categories. As the title implies, they are special for they offer a uniqueness or a specialty. Their duties should be confined to their area of specialization so that their services would be available to more than one teacher.

The classification of special aides should be reserved for those who do have a mutually agreed upon and recognized special talent or proficiency in a specific field.

Special aides should be recommended for employment and deployment by the local educational association's aide selection committee to prevent open-ended teacher aide exploitation.

What Type and How Much In-Service Training Should Special Aides Have?

To predetermine an inclusive overall training program for special aides would be foolish because the special aide category finds persons from all walks of life, each possessing certain unique abilities, insights, or talents which can be enhancing to our youth. However, it must be remembered that the same degree of educational proficiency and sophistication are not the qualifying criteria.

Uniqueness, insight, and special talent are the qualifying criteria, with no mention of education or experience commonality. Due to the qualifying discrepancies, it is necessary for the local

---

[4] *The National School Volunteer Program,* Public Education Association, 24 W. 40th Street, New York, New York.

education association to decide on each aide individually and to determine under whose jurisdictional sanction each aide belongs.

The first training problem to be resolved is that of individually determining the specific role for which each special aide has been employed. If their deployment is to be menial or clerical, their training could be of narrow scope, short duration and under the sanction of the local educational association. If special aides are to be used in roles dealing with the students or community members directly and actively, comprehensive and specific training should be required in compliance with the State Department of Education Certification Code.

What Duties Could Special Teacher Aides Perform?

By definition, special aides are persons from all walks of life who possess certain unique abilities, insights or talents which yield educational rewards in the schools. Criteria for special aides should not be rigid qualifying factors such as educational attainment, but the possession of the unique abilities, talents and insights. Although employment practices in regards to qualifications may be relaxed to accommodate the special aides, actual deployment must comply strictly with the adopted guidelines.

Contemporary practices involving the use of special aides are as expansive as the educational curricula. A few of the more widely known and practiced special aide categories are: [5]

Classroom Aide
    performs clerical, monitorial, and teacher re-enforcement tasks under the direct supervision of the classroom teacher.

---

[5] *Paraprofessionalism in the Schools of Wayne County, Michigan*, Report of the Paraprofessional Study, ESEA Title III, Wayne County Intermediate School District, Detroit, Michigan, September, 1968, p. 16-17.

Audio-Visual Technician
inventories, stores, performs simple maintenance tasks, and operates audio-visual equipment; may also assist as a stage manager.

School Counselor's Aide
performs clerical, monitorial, and counseling re-enforcement tasks under the direction of the counselor.

School Lunchroom Aide
supervises lunchroom according to school practices during lunch periods; maintains order, helps children when assistance is needed, works with administration and teachers to improve procedures; supervises after-lunch playground or special activities.

General School Aide
performs a variety of school duties as assigned by principal, assistant principal, or designated teacher; may assist at doors and in halls, office, bookstore, library, clinic, classroom, but is not assigned to a single station.

School Community Aide
acts as a liaison person between the school and the community to inform parents of school and community services and to inform teachers of community problems and special needs.

School Hospitality Aide
receives parents who visit the school and, under the direction of the principal, conducts the parent to where the parent may meet with a teacher; may also arrange for refreshments for teachers, parents, and for children.

Departmental Aide
works in a particular school department (language, science, fine arts, etc.) to perform designated departmental tasks

such as record keeping, inventories, attendance, supplies, marking objective tests, etc.

Library Aide

works under the supervision of the certificated librarian to assist in operation of the school library. Shelving, filing, clipping, circulation, and book processing are some of the tasks to be performed. Helps students find books and reference materials.

Testing Service Aide

works with professional testers in schools or regional centers to arrange for, administer, check, and record student test results.

Teacher Clerical Aide

performs record keeping function, collecting, monitoring, duplicating of tests and school forms.

School Security Aide

assigned by the principal to security tasks—doors, corridors, special events, lavatories, parking lot, banking of school receipts.

After-school Program Aide

supervises, under the direction of the teacher, any after-school activities.

Materials Resource Center Assistant (Program Learning Lab Assistant)

performs clerical, custodial, and monitorial functions in a material resource center or program learning laboratory.

Special Talent Paraprofessional

has special talents to assist teacher in teaching art, music, and/or crafts.

Special Skills Aide

assists teacher by having special skills in the areas of shop, homemaking, or speaking a foreign language.

Crisis Center Paraprofessional (Opportunity Room)
works with children who have problems of adjustment in the regular classroom situation.

Playground (Recreation) Paraprofessional
works with teachers during the school day to assist with physical education activities.

Reading Improvement Aide
assists reading specialist with basic and/or remedial instruction in a single school or group of schools; reads stories or serves as a listener.

Special Education Aide
assists special education teacher in implementing instruction and activities for individual or groups of special education pupils.

Speech Correction Aide
works with speech correction teacher to provide increased correctional services for pupils with speech problems.

Attendance Officer Aide
provides assistance in dealing with attendance problems; may make home calls whose purpose is delineated by the attendance officer.

Bus Attendant Aide
is employed at beginning and end of the school day to supervise loading and unloading of school buses; may be assigned to ride buses, especially those transporting very young children. Help with field trip activities and supervision.

High School Theme Reader
reads and checks class themes for those aspects of writing indicated by the teacher.

School Health Clinic Aide
operates health clinic under direction provided by school nurse.

Laboratory Technician

assists in school laboratories (language, science) under supervision of teacher; sets up, maintains, and operates equipment.

Enrichment Opportunity Aide
provides general and additional in-depth tutorial or personalized assistance.

What are Practical Aides?

A practical aide can be any person who, in the opinion of the aide selection committee, has qualities conducive to the overall betterment of the educational program. The duties of the practical aide should be confined to either very narrow specialties or the more menial and clerical duties.

What Type and How Much Training Should Practical Aides Have?

Practical aides should have a high school diploma or the equivalent.

In-service training for practical aides should be required. At least one hour per school week should be allotted to planned training, orientation and consultation.

Prior to the fall opening of school, all practical aides should be required to spend one full week (40 hours) in basic orientation and training.

What Duties Could be Performed by Practical Aides?

Practical aides should be able to perform all functions required of the student, mother and father aides. In addition, practical aides should be able to perform the following functions:

1. Give extra help to students who do not understand assignments.

2. Assist students with difficult information, pertinent information on missed assignments and make-up work.

3. Record data on the cumulative records.

4. Correct and grade assignment papers, workbooks, and reports and projects.

5. Correct objective tests.

6. Score and profile achievement and diagnostic tests.

7. Serve as a laboratory assistant.

8. Serve as an instructional and project demonstrator.

9. Conduct reading, spelling, etc. groups.

10. Serve as a proctor.

11. Average academic marks.

12. Complete school and county reports.

13. Supervise the class when the teacher must leave.

14. Keep attendance records.

15. Telephone parents on routine matters such as verifying notes for requests to leave school early, or to check on student absences.

16. Help to prepare school newspaper materials.

17. Enter grades into teacher's record book.

18. Supervise club meetings.

19. Arrange for and supervise indoor games on rainy days.

20. Prepare introductions to Audio-Visual materials to provide students with background in either using or viewing them.

21. Escort injured or sick students home who have no telephone or transportation.

22. Escort an injured or sick child to a doctor or hospital.

23. Conduct tutorials with individuals or small groups.

24. Decorate the classroom or auditorium for special occasions.

These duties are not all-inclusive, nor are they meant to serve as a permissive or restrictive guide in the deployment of practical aides. However, these duties do point out the magnitude and type of responsibilities that could be proficiently performed by this aide category. The type of duties outlined do not violate or degrade educational ethics in any way.

What are Certified Aides?

A certified aide is semi-qualified, with at least one year of formalized post-high school training. The State Department of Education should certify this type of aide.

Certification should allow for performance in semi-instructional classroom activities, while working under the direct supervision of a certified teacher.

How Much and What Type of Training Should Certified Aides Have?

The requirement for becoming a certified aide should be at least fivefold:

1. Have completed at least one year or 30 semester hours of post high school training. This training should be in educational areas deemed pertinent to the enhancement of a quality performance as a teacher aide.

2. Serve at least a one-year internship as a practical aide or have proven equivalent experience. The waivering of the internship for past experience should be determined and approved by the State Department of Education.

3. Interns should be recommended for promotion to certified aides by their past supervising teacher or teachers. Recommendations should also be mandatory for certified aides being hired on an experience waiver.

4. Should be given official sanction by the local education association.

5. All newly certified aides should be required to spend one week in orientation and training prior to the opening of school in the fall. Following this, weekly scheduled in-service training sessions of not less than one hour's duration should be mandatory. Weekly sessions could be with the supervising teacher or in some other planned activity, either individualized or grouped.

What Duties Could be Performed by Certified Aides?

Certified aides should be allowed to perform all the duties which are required of student, mother, father, and practical aides. Additional duties that certified aides should be able to perform are:

1. Lead the class or a group in simple comprehensive, skill, appreciation or drill exercises.

2. Tutor individual students.

3. Brief students on missed or misunderstood instructions.

4. Preview and report on films and other audio-visual aides.

5. Proofread and edit student copy for student newspapers.

6. File correspondence and other reports in student records.

7. Obtain special material for special class projects.

8. Supervise various auxiliary school projects.

9. Organize and supervise intramural activities and programs.

10. Assist or direct skits and plays.

11. Teach and emphasize good conduct and etiquette.

12. Assist students with the basic writing skills, such as composition, grammar, punctuation.

13. Arrange field trips, collect parental permission forms, insure correct scheduling, inform students of safety and dress regulations.

14. Administer first aid, care for and remain with an injured or ill student.

15. Confer with teachers and/or the principal regarding specific students.

16. Conduct certain routine classroom activities.

17. Assist the teacher in developing and organizing classroom material.

18. Assist teachers with basic research problems.

19. Observe students and report exaggerated behavior, both positive and negative, to the teacher.

20. Serve as a substitute teacher when the regular teacher is absent.

Should Certified Aides Serve as Substitute Teachers?

Yes . . . . . For years our educational system has employed thousands of pseudo-teachers who have less than two years of post high school training. Thousands more have been regularly employed after acquiring two years of college training. Many school systems are still forced to use non-degree teachers.

Generally, educators agree that substitute teachers are most often strictly a holding action. As a group, substitute teachers are the least capable of coping with varying classroom climates. It is unrealistic to believe that substitute teachers are able, at best, to bring anymore than a facsimile of course continuity and progress to the classroom.

Why not use certified aides as substitute teachers? Certified aides are natural substitutes because they are:

1. Acquainted with the students.

2. A part of and a participant in the day-to-day developments of the classroom.

3. Aware of the teacher's aims and objectives.

4. Able to eliminate the basic confusion and disorder connected with substitute teachers.

5. Familiar with the school and classroom routines.

These are just a few of the reasons why certified aides could efficiently serve as substitute teachers. However, in order to prevent both the teachers and the aides from being exploited, basic rules should be set up and rigidly adhered to.

How Should Certified Aides, Serving as Substitute Teachers, be Regulated?

Certified aides serving as substitute teachers should be subject to the following regulations:

1. Must have valid certification.

2. Should be permitted to teach only in classes or classrooms in which they are regularly employed.

3. Must have the recommendation of the supervising teacher as to capabilities and responsibility.

4. Be permitted to serve only in the cases where the teacher's absence is caused by illness or days covered by the teacher's professional absence days.

5. Be limited to approximately 24 teaching days per year, based on the possibility of substituting for two teachers for whom the aide may regularly assist, allowing for 10 sick days and two professional leave days per year per teacher.

6. Be sanctioned for this type of substitute teaching by the local educational association.

What are Reader and Grader Aides?

Reader and grader aides are those who are used only to check compositions for errors in capitalization, punctuation, spelling, sentence structure, word usage, and basic theme organization. These aides may comment on how basic composition could be improved.

Reader aides could also be used for grading vocabulary tests, written drills, extra work, special projects and objective tests. They should be able to recommend letter grades for all paper content passing before them. However, all grade approval should remain with and be the direct responsibility of the teacher.

Reader and grader aides may or may not have assigned work stations at the schools. Most of a reader aide's work can be assigned and taken home. The scheduling of hours for reader and grader aides can be flexible enough to fit almost any individual situation.

A reader aide, generally speaking, would be required to have a college degree. Exceptions to a college degree could be made, but only in rare and well-qualified instances.

Heavy emphasis and preference should be given to those who have a major in English.

Aside from the educational requirement, the screening process should include successful completion of a standardized language proficiency test, in addition to an oral interview dealing primarily with both the understanding of and cooperation with youth and skill developing philosophies.

A lay reader should not be appointed until he has met all of the requirements of the screening process. To allow the use of unqualified personnel as lay readers is an unwise practice. This aide category is highly subject to and often suspect of nepotismic practices. To assume that a person will automatically be a good lay reader because of past occupational positions or of professional "renown," is foolhardy. The screening process as outlined is a device that not only insures against nepotism but also gives dignity to this educational practice.

A study of lay reader programs in 30 California districts showed 19 districts thought the program contributed a "great deal" to the improvement of student writing, 10 reported "some improvement," and one district noted "very little" improvement.[6]

Insist that lay readers be fully qualified.

What Type and How Much In-service Training Should Reader and Grader Aides Have?

Reader and grader aides should be required to attend an orientation session to acquaint them with staff members and orient them to their new duties, expectations and responsibilities.

At least one follow-up session should also be required to cover any missed or misunderstood points of the initial orientation session. Periodic planned visits between the teachers and their reader-grader aides are highly recommended as an ongoing requirement for employment.

It is important that reader and grader aides are available and able to make occasional visits to the school. The overall success of this type teacher-teacher aide involvement is highly dependent upon harmonious working relationships and open communication channels. Scheduled and consistent follow-up and guidance conferences for all lay readers and graders should be considered a must.

It is the teacher's responsibility to see that a standard set of evaluative and corrective marking symbols are provided for and understood by both students and aides. Teachers should also inform the aides as to what type of errors to look for and of the basic philosophy behind each type of assignment.

---

[6] Marilyn H. Cutler, "Teacher Aides Are Worth the Effort," *Nation's Schools*, April, 1964, p. 67-69, p. 116-118.

A successful reader-grader aide program will not allow either the teacher or the aide to completely divorce themselves from any delegated tasks.

What Duties Could Lay Reader and Grader Aides Perform?

Reader and grader aides should be able to perform the following duties:

1. Make helpful and corrective notes on students' written work.

2. Suggest to students ways to improve their work and recommend specific resource materials.

3. Hold tutorial conferences with individual students.

4. Recommend writing and outline techniques.

5. Be sure that the teacher is aware of evidence pointing to student and course content deficiencies.

6. Express, to the supervising teacher, personal views and observations regarding improvement of corrective markings or techniques.

7. Conduct remedial classes and act as an outside resource person.

8. Supervise student make-up assignments and extra duty.

9. Serve as a consultive resource person for the teacher.

10. Conduct group indoctrination sessions on phases of writing and forms of expression.

In order for a reader-grader aide program to operate successfully, the teacher must give these aides:

1. Status both within and without the classroom.
2. Freedom to act in a receptive environment.

3. Responsibility for their actions.
4. An attentive ear.
5. Individual respect.
6. Background information when needed.
7. Proper support.
8. Guidance that will allow aides to operate with empathy and enthusiasm.

An uncoordinated and uncommitted teacher-reader-grader aide combination is a serious injustice to the entire educational operation.

A reader-grader aide should be given student visibility and personal contact for an unseen aide can easily and unintentionally become a scapegoat and be viewed as an impersonal mechanistic operation.

Do not create a void between teacher-teacher aide or teacher aide-student.

CHAPTER VIII

SELECTION OF TEACHER AIDES

At some time or other, everyone passes judgment on someone or something. Yet the process of true and sound evaluation, involving as it does the weighing of truth against sound values, demands intelligence and mature thought.

Winifred E. Bain

Selection of Teacher Aides

How Should Aides be Selected and who Should be Selected for Aide Employment?

Many aide employment selection methods are currently being used. No one method would best serve all school system needs. What has been proven a beneficial and sound method in one district may prove an unsound practice in a neighboring district. Each aide selection and employment program should be individually planned and tailored to fit the needs of the district it serves.

According to the finding of research conducted by the New York State Teachers Association, 83 per cent of the state districts surveyed who are employing teacher aides reported that the job of selection was done by one or more members of the administrative staff, with teachers and administrators acting cooperatively in 7 per cent of the districts. It also reported that more than 50 per cent of the district's methods of hiring and deployment duties of aides were at the suggestion of the administrator.

However, individual teachers and teacher groups did cooperatively plan with the administration in about 41 per cent of the cases studied. Cooperative planning efforts resulted in teachers either initiating employing plans or developing guidelines for employment practices.

Before any type teacher aide program can be logically planned or initiated the following conditions must be met:

The type or types of aide program(s) to be initiated must be specified.

The legality of the program in regard to state statutes must be insured.

Consent of school board must be obtained.

Administrative consent, along with basic employment and deployment guidelines and philosophy, must be obtained.

Kind and amount of sanctioned cooperation given the program by the local education association must be assured.

Secondary factors that should be taken into account are:

1. having an informed teaching staff

2. having the Parent-Teacher Association be aware of the teacher aide program and its involvement

3. have local newspapers and communication sources informed as to the general teacher aide operation plans

4. inform social and civic groups of the teacher aide programs, regarding their operation, involvement and purpose.

The employment and deployment of all teacher aide personnel should be the responsibility of the district school administrator.

He, in turn, should delegate authority to sub-administrators or to the local education association to carry out the tasks involved. The choice of aide administration should be primarily determined by the prevailing local structure and conditions.

There are many favorable reasons for aide supervision by the local education association and also for live administrative control. Regardless of who has the vested authority to employ aides, all employment must be predicated on planned deployment.

Therefore, the supervising teacher who is expected to work with and be responsible for the aide would be involved in the selection process. This teacher should be allowed the privilege and given the responsibility of interviewing the aide applicant assigned to her for approval or disapproval. To give added assurance to the aide program's success, the supervising teacher must have an active role in the aide selection process. To arbitrarily make aide assignments could be disastrous and render the program ineffective.

For What Type of Qualities Should all Teacher-Aide Aspirees be Screened?

All aides must unequivocally and without question possess high standards of mental and moral turpitude. Each aide should be required to show current proof of a negative tuberculin test (Shick test, X-Ray). Paid aides should also be required to pass a routine physical examination. It would be desirable to have volunteer aides pass a routine physical examination.

When interviewing and recruiting, either paid or volunteer aides, the following qualities should be noted and emphasized:

1. willingness to accept responsibility

2. fondness for children

3. patience and tolerance

4. friendliness

5. restraint from use of crude or abusive language

6. restrained philosophy on the use of physical force and coercion

7. cooperativeness

8. honesty, integrity, and sincerity

9. respect for individual differences and personal worth

10. appropriate philosophies on empathy, apathy, authority, and permissiveness

11. appropriate manner of dress and general personal neatness

12. restraint of personal bias and prejudice

13. personal points of contention and areas of criticism

14. philosophy of leadership and/or followership

15. demonstrated sensitivity to the needs of youth

16. ability to work with a teacher

17. ability to work with various school personnel

In the final evaluation the interviewer should ask himself: "Is this the type of person I would want to be in a position to exert adult influence on my child?"

These critical areas should be thoroughly investigated when selecting aides. A strong, effective teacher aide program is not the result of good fortune, but only the result of good planning.

What Degree of Proficiency Should be Expected or Required of Teacher Aides?

Contemporary practices on the employment and deployment of teacher aides are as numerous as the supervising imaginations involved.

Two unique teacher aide programs which outline qualifications and deployment rationale are:

1. David H. Goldstein, executive director of the Indianapolis Pre-school Center, Inc., reported on the use of 40 teacher aides, each assigned to a classroom.

   Many of the teacher aides were receiving public assistance, were indigenous to the immediate area, and most had less than a 10th grade education. These aides primarily served a six-fold purpose:

   1. to bridge the gap and encourage shy parents to directly approach the teacher

   2. to interpret the environmental conditions and mores of the community to the teachers in order for them to better understand various problems

   3. to serve as a liaison person by making the initial home visit

   4. to serve as a substitute person when the regular teacher is not able to be present

   5. to be the adult-confidant of the pupils and to communicate the students' desires and an interpretation of their problems to the teacher

   6. to serve as an individual or small group tutor. [1]

---

[1] David H. Goldstein, Executive Director of the Indianapolis Pre-School Center, Inc., Indiana, *The Instructor*, October, 1966.

2. "Cops in the classroom" reports on the use of uniformed police as teacher aides. The rationale is that bringing police officers into the classroom on a regular basis would improve juvenile social attitudes. Hopefully, the pupils would see their uniformed teacher aides as representatives of what is necessary, good and desired in our society. [2]

Under the auspices of the Wayne County Intermediate School District, the Paraprofessional Study, Title III, ESEA, USOE, No. 67-2998 was conducted in the district. Within the 622 square miles of the district at the time of the study were 708,000 school children in 43 local school districts. The school districts ranged in size from the city of Detroit with 296,089 pupils and 9,946 teachers to the Brownstown Township School District No. 10 with 104 pupils and 7 teachers.

There are 33 major city and township units of government. Wayne County has an estimated population of 2,728,000 which is greater than the population of 30 of the United States. Nearly one-third of Michigan's school population is in the area served by the Wayne County Intermediate Office of Education, although there are demographic extremes in the county ranging from the densely populated urban Detroit to sparse rural communities only a few miles away. (See chart page 157.)

From What Sources and how Should Teacher Aides be Sought?

Although children are sent to school for an education, the prime educators are the parents themselves. In order to achieve

---

[2] Daniel Malvesta and Eugene L. Ronayne, "Cops in the Classroom," *NEA Journal*, December, 1967.

HOW PARAPROFESSIONALS FUNCTION IN
WAYNE COUNTY PUBLIC SCHOOLS

School District	Classroom	Counselor	Adm.	General School	Library	Other
Allen Park	X					
Carson					X	
Dearborn Heights No. 7					X	
Dearborn No. 8 Fr.						X
Ecorse	X					
Brownstown No. 10				X	X	
Detroit	X	X	X	X	X	X
Grosse Ile	X				X	
Hamtramck	X	X			X	
Harper Woods					X	
Heintzen	X				X	X
Highland Park	X				X	
Huron					X	X
Inkster	X			X		X
Lincoln Park	X				X	X
Livonia	X			X	X	X
Maple Grove				X		
Melvindale					X	X
Nankin Mills					X	
Northville				X	X	
Plymouth	X					
River Rouge	X					
Romulus				X		
Southgate						X
South Redford						X
Trenton	X	X	X			
Wayne	X				X	

a balance between home and school, the ideals and the objectives of the parents must be identified with those of the school lest a two-phased dichotomy be created.

To create this balance the school must reach into the home and the home into the school. This can be done effectively by bringing the parents into the school as teacher aides. This gives parents and teachers a firsthand opportunity to gain a knowledge of each other's ideals and objectives as well as an understanding of the means used to attain them. [3]

If we are assured that parents are an ideal source of teacher aides, the problem becomes one of recruitment.

When the teacher aide program is in the planning stage, the parents should be sent an explanatory letter concerning the nature and means of the program. Included with this letter could be a form by which parents may indicate their interest in participating in the program, a brief background summary including education and work experience. The form may also include a proposed list of teacher aide categories including functions of each and the days and hours which are available for teacher aide assistance. [4]

The P.T.A. is a great source of teacher aides and should be tapped because it usually abounds with parents eager to help broaden the scope of school activities. Not only are the members of the P.T.A. parents, but they have also expressed a direct concern with educational advancement by membership in the P.T.A.

Although the parent pool is a major source of teacher aides, it is but one of many.

---

[3] Sister Phyllis Boudreau, C.N.D., "Teacher Aides," NCEA Bulletin, August, 1967.
[4] Ibid.

Retirees are often willing and able to contribute their service. Not only do these citizens aide the students but they also give significance to their own lives.

College students, particularly those in education, are often eager to work in community projects. Many specifically desire the practical experience of working with children. Statistically, college students are the largest source of volunteers.

Retired teachers frequently would like to get back into the school, but with less of the planning, paperwork and hours required of a full-time teacher. Present teachers may elect to become teacher aides for the same reasons. However, regularly employed teachers should be carefully screened—they must be ready and able to give full authority to the full-time professionally employed teacher. These ex-teachers must realize that they are no longer in command.

Every community has large pools of local aide personnel. Community leaders may be willing to devote a few hours a week just for a change of pace. A local artist or musician may be willing to help local students explore the arts under competent, skilled hands.

Active or former scout leaders and Sunday school teachers may be willing to work with groups in the school during the school day.

A desirable aide is any person who has talent, whether it be artistic or merely patience and warmth. There are no restrictions on age, sex, race, ecomomic or educational background. Aides are everywhere, but it is up to the schools to interest potential aides and bring them into the schools.

There should not be a standardized method of recruitment or selection for school systems are by no means standardized. Each system must individualize recruitment and selection procedures on the basis of the needs of the community schools.

159

The people are available, the problem is communicating the need for aides to the people who desire to assist. Methods of communicating this need are:[5]

1. Holding a public meeting to discuss the teacher aide program and the liberal qualifications for the employment of aides.

2. Have all conferences well-publicized in local newspapers.

3. Send bulletins to community agencies, organizations, and businesses to alert them to the need for aides and the desire for aide applicants.

4. Send flyers home with school children.

5. Have posters and attractive displays concerning the aide program in store windows, churches and schools and public buildings.

6. Arrange speaking engagements with community organizations such as men's and women's clubs, veteran's and church groups and all local P.T.A. units.

Although low-income groups include many parents, recruitment should give special attention to this group. Government programs have made funds available for the training and salaries of teacher aides, which enables many low-income people to increase their training and skills, raise their income and hence social position in society. This also enables persons in low-income groups to become significant members of their community.

Who Should Determine the Amount and Type of Training Aides Should be Required to Complete?

The training or indoctrination of ELEMENTARY or SECONDARY SCHOOL STUDENT AIDES, MOTHER

---

[5] Ibid.

AIDES, FATHER AIDES, and PRACTICAL AIDES should be the responsibility of the local school administration. The administrators in turn can delegate to the local education association the authority to determine the type and amount of training required.

The training requirements for CERTIFIED AIDES and READER AIDES should be the responsibility of the State Department of Education.

The categories of VOLUNTEER AIDES and SPECIAL AIDES should be subject to strict role interpretation and dealt with according to planned deployment, either locally or at the state level.

Employing schools are ever fearful of not having a sound legal base on which to employ teacher aides. In this matter, school systems become defensive and seek ways to defend their action and legally justify teacher aides.

School boards and administrators are equally fearful of losing state reimbursement monies for educational practices which are sanctioned by the state or professional educational organizations.

Regardless of need and pertinence to the situation, the pressure to justify is real, however unwarranted. If there is a need and the need is valid, corrective action to facilitate justification should be initiated through the proper channels. (The states must first set the certification guidelines and limits of the teacher aides' duties.) Then the various professional teaching organizations must also determine what they feel is justifiable and in the interest of professional growth.

Once this is done, each school district must determine, according to its need and the expressed desire of its supervising teachers, what can be done in teacher aide placement. Each of the three steps outlined must be taken into account and the autonomy of each must be recognized.

Should There be an Educational Ceiling Placed on Those Applying for Teacher Aide Positions?

The amount of post high school educational training a person has should not serve as the sole restrictive clause in prohibiting their employment as teacher aides. Each case should be considered on its own merits and dealt with accordingly.

School working conditions and the typical school calendar make the aide job attractive, convenient and desirable. There are many reasons why well-qualified personnel will desire to serve as a teacher aide. Former teachers who do not wish to teach full-time may fill special teacher aide slots very well. Others may accept a nonprofessional role with long-range professional objectives in mind.

It is wise to question the motives of a well-qualified person who is seeking an aide position. The teacher must feel secure, undisturbed and unchallenged by the other adult in her classroom. Not everyone who has experienced leadership can revert to a passive, follower role.

Should People Indigenous to a Particular Environment be Given Preference in the Hiring of Teacher Aides?

Yes . . . . . personnel indigenous to a community are a source of assets to both the classroom and the school. Aides from similar backgrounds to that of the parents and students are able to perceive, discuss, and deal with the people and the problems of the area in a more informed manner.

A teacher of a school system can easily heighten or diminish various school problems according to the referent value system used. This might be particularly true in disadvantaged neighborhoods where indigenous persons may be able to have more rapport with and sensitivity to the students and parents than the teachers or the school community are able to develop.

However, being indigenous to a community should not be the sole criteria for aide employment regardless of the community. Each aide hired should in all cases be able to immediately or have the potential to make a significant contribution to the employing educational program.

Indigenous aides interpreting community mores are able to give educators meaningful and realistic insights in which to temper their judgments and actions. However, aides cannot infuse education with a sense of reality if the school system and teacher have an unrealistic sense of their students' total environment.

The greater the deviation from the middle class value system, either upward or downward, the greater the need for employing indigenous aides.

A properly selected and trained aide indigenous to a community would be helpful in inspiring teachers to provide a more meaningful and effective learning environment.

Should Persons on Welfare and Relief Roles be Assigned to Work as Teacher Aides?

They should be hired only if the initial planning allows and provides accordingly for them to become a part of the overall operation.

However, no person should be hired as an aide just because he is poor or unemployed. Regardless of the type of aide category, each aide should be employed strictly on the basis of merit and ability to make a worthwhile contribution to some part of the educational program.

Just being·a poor and available person, and indigenous to a given community, is not sufficient criteria for being hired as a teacher aide at any categorical level.

Should Persons With low Income or Persons on Welfare or Relief Roles be Given Preference in the Selection of Teacher Aides?

Such persons should be given preference only if the program is designed to include them and provide for meaningful and beneficial deployment. To have merit, aide programs must be fabricated upon sound values and dignity, with regard for intrinsic personal self-worth. It is insidious as well as unscrupulous to hire adult bodies simply to fill allotted space in the educational system. A well-structured, detailed program involving low and negative income adults has merit for all concerned.

No one should be hired or accepted solely on the basis of providing the needy with a job. Whenever anyone is employed in the capacity of a teacher aide, it should be with the firm belief that he can and will make a worthwhile contribution to the educational program.

Stereotyping the poor, ignorant or indigent has occasionally caused the aide program some unfavorable comments and temporary set-backs. However, there is no valid reason to disqualify a person as a potential aide for any category for which he is qualified solely on the basis of his economic status.

It has been shown that utilization of a person who has struggled through social problems to cope with similar problems has yielded worthwhile results.

Thus far, the largest potential pool of sub-professional talent, has been in the low-income group, which has supplied teacher's aides under recent educational programs for combating poverty.

In addition, America's low-income areas, where the need to improve schooling is critical, have benefited most from the use of aides in their schools. In the summer of 1964 some 46,000 teacher aides were used in preschool programs, in low income areas, throughout the country.[6]

---

[6] William J. Rioux, "At The Teacher's Right Hand," *American Education*, December 1965-January 1966, p. 5-6.

CHAPTER IX

AIDE TRAINING

The function of organization is to set the stage and to facilitate the application in the classroom of the kind of education one desires for children and the method whereby children may get it.

Henry J. Otto, *Elementary School Organization and Administration* (Appleton-Century and Crofts, 1954).

Aide Training

Is it an Absolute Necessity That all Teacher Aides be Given Some Training or Indoctrination?

Yes . . . . . All aides, regardless of duties or assignments, should be required to attend at least two in-service training sessions.

The first session should be devoted to introduction and indoctrination. Emphasis of this session should be on the school's basic educational objectives and policies and the manner in which the aides themselves will be involved.

The second session should follow within a month, not sooner than two weeks nor later than four weeks. This session should primarily be planned to answer the "whys," "whats," "wheres," "what fors," "whos," and "whens" of the aides.

Past teacher aide experience should be discussed with consideration for future courses of action. If the action of the group requires follow-up information, the in-service training resources involved should provide this service. Accurate and fast follow-up action with direct communication must be given first priority in all aide training programs.

No aide should be expected to perform at peak efficiency from the start. Aides must be indoctrinated or trained in accordance with their future school role involvement.

Why Should all Aides be Required to Undergo Basic Teacher Aide Training?

Since harmony in working relationships is so important, guidelines for the actions of both teachers and aides must be set up. All aides, regardless of their capacity, will benefit from both pre-training and in-service follow-up training. Points to be stressed in aide indoctrination and follow-up are: 1) Professionalism . . . . all aides will have varying amounts of access to privileged professional information. Therefore, it is necessary that they be reminded that they must operate on the same basis of ethics as the teaching profession. 2) Behavior . . . . exemplary behavior on the part of the aide is certainly important. 3) Cooperation . . . . team work and harmony are vital to the success of the program. 4) Punctuality . . . . educational activities are generally time oriented and punctuality is a basic key to success. 5) Responsibility . . . . to explain all of the encompassing demands and types of responsibilities found in a school system.

Each aide must be made aware of the fact that, once he is identified with school service and the teaching profession, he must assume the responsibilities of his new role. The aide is required to adopt a standard of behavior commensurate with his position and worthy of respect from the teachers, the students, and the community.

Should all Aides be Required to Have Approximately the Same Amount of Formalized Training?

No . . . . the strength of any teacher aide program rests primarily in its local acceptance and secondly in its employment and deployment diversity. The categorical placement versatility of aides should encourage teachers to use their imagination, rather than relying on or being tied to a structured order.

What is the Educational Background of Contemporary Teacher Aides?

A New England Study prepared by the New England Educational Assessment Project in 1965 revealed that five per cent of the teacher aides in the study had less than a high school diploma. Fifty-two per cent have been graduated from secondary school. Twenty-nine per cent have attended college and fourteen per cent have a degree.

Teacher aides participating in the study were grouped by the grades in which they were working: elementary, 1399 or 81%; secondary, 190 or 11%; elementary and secondary, 135 or 8%.

Educational Background of Teacher Aides
and Employment Level

Highest Grade Completed	Percent Employed in Elementary School	Percent Employed in Secondary School
Attended Secondary School	5	1
Graduated from Secondary School	48	34
College 1 year	11	14
College 2 years	11	16
College 3 years	4	3
Graduated from College	10	28
No Response	11	4

The New England Educational Assessment Project, A Cooperative Regional Project of the Six New England States, 1967, page 8.

171

Why are Teacher Aide Training Programs Necessary and What are the Various Types?

A study by the American Association of School Administrators indicated that only 16 of 229 systems participating in a nation-wide survey reported no formal training for teacher aides.[1] In 177 systems, or approximately 82 percent, the training of aides after employment was the responsibility of the classroom teacher.[2]

If aides are to make their fullest contribution to school programs their tasks must be clearly defined to provide maximum service by avoiding confusion and misunderstanding. The teacher aide training program must be task oriented and based on clearly delineated performance goals and should provide training experience to meet the goals. The training program must be preceded by the careful listing of the specific, observable goals which the aide is expected to meet. Training experiences should then be calculated to meet the goals.

Training should have a multi-level approach to meet the needs of central office administrators, principals, teachers and the aides. Such an approach demands flexibility of grouping in team sessions, grouping by professional level, grouping by aide function and other combinations of such grouping in work sessions, small group discussions and seminars.

A *work experience program* allows a trainee to achieve techniques and practices which have relevance to a particular job assignment. Learning by doing is directly applied on the job in role playing and job-simulation techniques.

---

[1] Education Research Service Circular No. 2, April, 1967, p. 9.

[2] Ibid.

Programmed materials such as those developed by Science Research, Inc., may be used by aides but should be supplemented with practical experience. The aide's independent study should be supervised by professionals of the team to insure understanding.

The following is an example of a training program of ten half-day sessions:[3]

1. "The Emerging Role of the Teacher Aide"
   General Session: Background
   Work Session: Bank College Checklist of activities, small groups
   General Summary: Reports of Work Sessions

2. Teacher Aide Work Session and Professional Seminar
   Audio-Visual Techniques Work Session
   Professionals will analyze and discuss twenty-six teacher aide job descriptions and performance tasks of aides.

3. Role-playing to involve all participants in teams and teams in combination; presentation of problems encountered in new staffing relationships
   General Summary: Symposium Report

4. Aide Work Sessions and Professional Seminar Work Sessions on large and small group games for children, and art activities. Aides learn by playing a variety of games and by engaging in the preparation of art projects and bulletin boards. Aide Trainee will analyze new staffing practices and how changes in staff affects classroom management.

---

[3] *The Practice and the Promise*, Paraprofessionalism in the Schools of Wayne County, Michigan, Report of the Paraprofessional Study, ESEA Title IV, Wayne County Intermediate School District, Detroit, Michigan, September. 1968.

5. Large and Small Aide Group Sessions and Professional Seminar. Aides will use films, micro-teaching demonstrations and SRI materials on the topic, "How Children Learn."

6. The Library and the Material Resource Center: introduction to material available at the library and other sources of materials.

7. Teacher Reenforcement Tasks in Reading, Writing, and Mathematics—school team approach. Practice in "how-to-do."

8. Sensitivity Training—The Dynamics of Groups Work, planned activities.

9. Large Group Work Sessions for Teacher Aides on Child Growth and Development—films and presentations with emphasis on nutrition.

10. The New Career Ladder, "Large and Small Group Discussion. Reaction Panel.

A *Formal in-service training program* for aides has been developed by the Union School District, Jackson, Michigan, to train aides to develop skills in working with students, teachers and the school staff. Training sessions for aides should include teachers and administrators to promote understanding of the common goals for the total program.

The program is planned to develop the aide's proficiency and to encourage personal development necessary for development of the role to be played in classroom human relations.

A formal in-service training program might include: [4]

1. Basic Communications: Primarily concerned with the fundamentals of grammar and composition. A unit

---

[4] . *A Look at Teacher Aides and Their Training*, Metropolitan Educational Research Association, Michigan State University, East Lansing, Michigan, 1968.

174

of penmanship including manuscript and cursive writing should be included.

2. Basic Mathematics: Simple computations and an introduction to the techniques of the new mathematics to allow the aide to become familiar with the course of study and the text and materials to be used.

3. Machine Operations and Audio-Visual Techniques: To develop skills in the use of the mimeograph, ditto, tape recorder, motion picture projector, slide projector and other audio-visual aides.

4. Child Development: A study of the growth and development of the elementary school child. A unit on the use and administration of standardized tests should be included.

5. Resource Centers: To acquaint the aide with the resources available.

6. Elementary School Procedure: To acquaint the aide with procedures involved in regard to scheduling, the building, records and other formal procedures and followed in the individual school.

Another in-service training program combines *on-the-job training* in various subject areas with teacher aide conferences, classroom experience and university-based courses in the behavioral sciences and education. Teacher aide conferences enable individual expressions of personal problems and questions of the aides.

Classroom experience focuses on an introduction to curriculum materials which will be used by the aide under teacher supervision. University courses emphasize the Psychology, Sociology and Biology of Child Development. The education core consists of development of skills in reading, language and communication, and mathematics.

This program as developed by the Training Center for Community Programs of the University of Minnesota is as follows: [5]

SUBJECT AREAS	TASKS
1. Reading	Flashcard drill; make up reading games direct creative reading games, such as puppet shows, card box TV skits, administration of group tests such as Metropolitan Reading Readiness
2. Mathematics	Small group drill teams and individual attention, look for specific problems for extra attention, play number games with the children
3. Social Studies	Obtain and prepare discussion material lead group discussions, assist on field trips, help children learn to use the library
4. Writing-Spelling	Assist children in mechanics, lead spelling games, tell and listen to stories, teach children to use the dictionary, prepare tapes and charts
5. Music	Teach and sing folk songs and dances, lead rhythm activities, help build a record library, if possible help children learn basic music theory
6. Art	Assemble materials, help with technical frustrations by having supplies on hand, encourage children, discuss the meaning of work *to child with child*

---

[5] Ibid, p. 9.

SUBJECT AREAS	TASKS
7. Physical Education	Consult with assigned physical education teacher and report to teacher, lead playground activities during recess
8. Community Involvement	Provide knowledge of family background of pupils, make home visits when necessary

Community colleges may be the best place to train teacher aides because of the faculty and facilities available and because proximity would promote free communication between school system and college which would insure that the aides were being trained to meet the specific needs of the community schools.

There are three types of formal junior college teacher aide training programs: a one-year certificate program, a two-year program granting an associate degree, and a two-year program which encourages an aide to continue her education to gain professional status as a certified teacher which insures the transferability of credit to a senior college.[6]

The *one-year program* offered at St. Petersburg Junior College is designed to "meet the needs of individuals for future employment as Teacher-Aides" and "provide special educational opportunities for the parents of young children."[7]

The curriculum for this program is:

First Semester

Child, Family, and Community
Basic Communications

---

[6] Ibid, p. 12.

[7] Ibid, p. 13.

Fundamental Math
Orientation to Education
General Psychology
Elementary Typing
Physical Education Activities

Second Semester

Child Development
Related Arts
Machine Operations
Science Experiments for Elementary Schools
Internships
Elementary Typing

A *one-year program* which leads to a *certificate* has been implemented at Aurora College, Aurora, Illinois. The program requires thirty semester hours of college credit. Fifteen of these hours must include core courses of Educational Psychology, Instructional Materials, Freshman English, Introduction to Psychology and Introduction to Sociology.

The remaining 15 hours must include at least three areas chosen from: Biology, Educations, English, General Education (Linguistics & Semantics), Geography, History, Mathematics, Music, Philosophy, Physical Education, Physics, Psychology and Sociology.

A *two-year "semi-professional" curriculum* is offered at the City College of San Francisco which offers a choice of either pre-kindergarten assisting or elementary school assisting. Both choices offer orientation in teacher assisting, childhood and adolescent psychology, life sciences, physical education for children, art, professional and community relationships, typing and first aid along with pre-kindergarten and elementary core courses.

The pre-kindergarten core consists of pre-kindergarten procedures and practices, nature study, and the child and the family. The elementary core consists of elementary school procedures and practices, use of the library, preparation of audio-visual materials and operation of audio-visual equipment and children's dramatics. [8]

Dramatizing the upward mobility aspect of the teacher aide is the *"New Careers" program.* [9] In this program anyone can enter the program and after minimal training, earn money on the job while learning. A continuing education-work program allows the aide to increase her earnings as she increased her level of training. Although the aide is not compelled to continue her education, the program does lead to certification, if she desires. The program also included many courses with college-transferable credit which serves as inducement for continuing education. [10]

Would Teacher In-Service Training be Feasible for Use of Teacher Aides?

When an aide enters a classroom the supervising teacher must realize that her job has taken on a new dimension—the teacher is now also a supervisor.

Teachers are oriented to performance without direct supervision and sometimes expect an aide to also be an independent worker, but because aides play a supportive role they should be considered as dependent personnel under the supervision of the professional teacher.

---

[8] *A Look at Teacher Aides and Their Training*, Metropolitan Educational Research Association, Michigan State University, East Lansing, Michigan, 1968, pp. 14-15.

[9] Ibid, p. 19.

[10] Ibid, p. 24.

Some teachers have not developed the managerial skills necessary for supervisory tasks and will require guidance and assistance in developing these skills. Teachers working with nonprofessional helpers, either in or out of classrooms, must rely upon their own professional judgment when assigning duties to nonprofessional helpers. The teacher should be able to distinguish which duties will not infringe upon her professional responsibilities but will allow the aide to help the teacher in meeting her responsibilities.

The teacher who has the assistance of an aide must be secure and undisturbed in her position by the presence of another adult in her classroom. In the past, teachers have not received training for supervision of other adults in the classroom, but the recent introduction of another adult in the classroom has indicated a need for instruction of teachers in supervisory principles and the implementation of auxiliary personnel.

Aides need explicit directions and appreciate them while trying to define their roles. Aides as well as teachers should not hesitate to ask the questions which clarify and strengthen their relationship, and teachers should not hesitate to make explicit requests which will assert authority but will also clarify the teacher-teacher aide relationship.

Teachers with newly acquired aides should have supervision and direction in aide usage to help her learn by doing. Assistance and consultation while adjusting to her new job of supervisor will help her to clarify her role and position, adjust to her new responsibilities and help her in developing a sound teacher-teacher aide relationship.

Who Should Assume the Responsibility of Training Auxiliary Personnel?

The major responsibility for training auxiliary personnel must lie within the local school system. Since school staff, particularly the teachers, will determine which roles the aides will have, they should take an active part in the aides' selection and training.

However, some one person must have the designated authority and responsibility for overseeing an adequate training program for teacher aides. The chief administrator is the most logical person within a school system to assume this responsibility.

By virtue of his position, a chief administrator is able to delegate functions as he deems advisable. The chief administrator is also the person held accountable for all consequences resulting from employment and deployment.

The following excerpt from the Bank Street College study further answers this question:

Administrators are not only chiefly responsible for establishing over-all goals and policies, setting the tone, and identifying what functions need to be performed and by whom; they are also responsible for implementing these decisions through fiscal operations and organizational procedures.

In the fiscal realm, uncertainty as to continued federal funding is a major problem. This uncertainty inhibits career development with its concomitants of a job sequence including graduated compensation, increments, and fringe benefits as well as work-study programs with remuneration for study and educational credit for work experience.

There are also many procedural matters to consider such as (1) matching the "right" kind of auxiliary with the "right" kind of teacher within an appropriate situation; (2) allowing teachers to volunteer to use auxiliaries, or at least to self-select them; (3) providing the opportunity to change partners with the minimum of sensitivity when the principal problem appears to be a clash of personality; and (4) scheduling time within the school day for the teacher-auxiliary teams to review their experiences in the classroom and plan together for the next day.

The role of administrator as interpreter to board, parents, and staff may seem burdensome to one who is not himself convinced of the ultimate values of auxiliaries to the school in coping with the complexities of the challenge.

Action Needed:

1. Assurance of continued funding by government as is unquestioned for roads and the maritime industry.

2. Priority in school budget "hard funds" for the employment and training of auxiliary personnel.

3. Close cooperation and joint planning by schools and local institutions of higher learning to develop work-study programs.

4. Orientation of administrators through institutional workshops involving professional associations, unions, and community agencies at some point in the discussion.

5. Additional personnel in each school to provide for administration and supervision of special projects, made possible by federal funding, such as projects for the use of auxiliary personnel.

6. A plan for career development in each school system.[11]

All training programs should also entail a systematic follow-up, including evaluation, description of the program in progress,

---

[11] Garda W. Bowman and Gordon J. Klopf, "New Careers and Roles in the American School." A study conducted for the Office of Economic Opportunity, New York: Bank Street College of Education, September, 1967, p. 36-37, p. 153-154.

interviews with participants, and continuing assistance for teacher aides. Crystalization of training programs should be avoided to promote continued use of evaluation results to aid in program improvement.

Who Should Train Advanced Teacher Aides?

The amount of training should be determined first by the type of aide being sought. Every educational institution engaged in training teacher aides must take into account the basic amount of educational exposure or experience required for entry employment.

Within the broad framework of aides, the needs and composition of groups of potential auxiliaries in various communities, the diverse policies of local school systems with respect to the utilization of auxiliaries, the available facilities and resources for training, and the nature and extent of cooperation in the institutional life of the area all have an impact on the training program.

Consideration should be given to future planning which would allow qualified and desiring entry teacher aides to gain a greater degree of educational proficiency.

In answer to the question of exactly which institutions should do the actual training, it should depend primarily upon the type and number of aides needed within a given area.

The initial research should deal with finding the real need for aides, then determine the initial number needed, the number needed annually for growth and replacement, the degree and amount of proficiency required for each, and the teacher aide acceptance both within and without the school.

If all seems favorable, step two would be to investigate and determine which educational institutions could serve the needs of each participating school district most expeditiously.

Five basic criteria should be researched and resolved by each participating school district before implementing final or binding action. These criteria are:

1. *Assessability* - This is an extremely important criteria due to environmental limitations, encompassing demands, and psychological restrictions placed upon many of the teacher aide aspirees.

2. *Availability* - This is simply a matter of determining just which training institutions are available and which can best meet the needs of each district. The term "availability" has many facets and each should be explored. First and foremost the administration of the institution should have a deep interest in the program. Physical facilities, teaching staff, consultive staff, follow-up staff, evaluative and curricula-making personnel and staff members providing ancillary services should be readily available to aide trainees.

3. *Desirability* - is basically an expressed, honest interest and concern for setting up and providing a teacher aide training program.

4. *Feasibility* - This criteria relates specifically to the type, content, and manner of program being set up. When researching various feasibility factors, automatic rechecks relating to other factors will be encountered, especially those related to availability.

5. *Reliability* - A self-explanatory term which in essence asks: What degree of full faith and credit can we place in the institutions in question to satisfactorily and proficiently perform the tasks assigned to them?

These five basic factors should be given a great deal of consideration when choosing teacher aide training institutions.

CHAPTER X

UTILIZING THE AIDE

The teacher is not always seen as a sort of all-purpose parent substitute or authority figure. In the eyes of many people he is also a specialist in the art of directing learning. This role, important in itself, is also an important ally to other roles the teacher may be asked to take on.

John M. Stephens, *The Psychology of Classroom Learning* (New York: Holt, Rinehart and Winston, Inc., 1965), p. 9.

Moreover, we should never forget that there may be human potentialities awaiting release and expression when we discover how to evoke them, especially by the care, nurture and education of children and youth.

Lawrence K. Frank in Association for Supervision and Curriculum Development, *New Insights and the Curriculum* (Washington, D.C.: the Association, 1963), p. 18.

Utilizing the Aide

Should Teacher Aides do More Than Wipe Noses, Clean up Messes, put on Galoshes, Oversee the Playground and Serve as Clerks?

Teacher Aides can significantly contribute to teachers, students, schools and their communities—if allowed to do so in a realistically structured program. It is also possible for an aide to enjoy herself and attain the personal satisfaction which results from the performance of a socially valuable service.

The teacher aide concept holds great promise in its built-in career ladder potential. The aide program holds hope of finding new, self-realizing jobs for thousands of unemployed or underemployed.

Underemployment is far more prevalent today than unemployment. Precautionary measures should be taken to insure that all aide employment is planned in accordance to realistic and acceptable deployment activities.

The following article by Thorwald Esbensen, in the January, 1966, Phi Delta Kappa editorial provides thought-provoking insights for aide usage.

"The primary purpose of teacher aides is to increase the effectiveness of the teacher in the classroom. If a plan is to be set up for the use of these aides, it is important to determine the nature of the duties to be performed. Are (aides) to do purely clerical and housekeeping tasks, or will they devote part of their time to assisting with the teaching function? If the former, noncertificated personnel can be employed. If the latter, the aide becomes a teacher. State statutes require that teachers must be certificated. The matter of primary concern here is not certification itself but the fact that certification implies preparation for teaching. Persons who perform professional, or even semiprofessional, duties must be properly prepared for them. While certification does not guarantee a successful teacher, it does attest to the completion of a program of preparation.

The prospect of having noncertificated personnel encroach upon the prerogatives of the regular teaching staff is certainly cause for legitimate concern. However, before we decide that any work which consists of "assisting with the teaching function" is automatically taboo for teacher aides, we ought to examine what it is that teacher education programs uniquely qualify our regular teachers to do.

In theory, at least, schools of education turn out teachers who are able *to arrange the formal learning environment in such a way that the goals of instruction are met.* The essential point is that the competent teacher must be capable of making certain kinds of *decisions.* The range and level of this decision making are what define the effective role of the classroom teacher.

Let's be more specific. A well-prepared teacher should be able to *determine* whether a certain instructional item may be usefully presented to a given student. The teacher does not necessarily have to *create* this item. The instructional material itself is normally available in commercially prepared form: books, films, records, tapes, filmstrips, and the like.

There is a common tendency to confuse teaching with producing and presenting. A particularly depressing example of this occurs in instructional television, which all too often consists of taped lectures with the camera obediently fixed on the speaker's mouth as it opens and closes on selected morsels of human wisdom. Thus we foster pseudo-innovation. The height of creativity consists in finding yet another way to chain some new marvel of communication to the presence of an educational broadcaster. We limit new media to what is essentially the traditional lecture decked out in mechanical finery.

As long as teaching is equated with specific overt activity, we shall spend a lot of time trying to decide which physical acts in themselves constitute teaching and which do not. The likely upshot of this will be the formulation of lists of approved and disapproved tasks for which teacher aides can be used. It would be difficult to suggest a more barren approach to the job of instruction.

Can we suppose, for example, that only the regular teacher should present any given body of information to a group of students? If so, what happens to the long-standing practice of using community resource persons to enrich the instructional program? Indeed, what happens to films, books, and other prime means of presenting information to students?

Can we reasonably maintain that the regular teacher is the only person qualified to 1) hear a child read the Dolch list of the ninety-five most common nouns, 2) read to children, 3) help students locate materials, 4) repeat directions concerning assignments?

Hardly. A competent teacher aide could do all of these things— each task clearly having the effect of "assisting with the teaching function."

We must conclude, I think, that the distinguishing characteristic of the qualified teacher is his ability to *analyze* the instructional needs of his students, and to *prescribe* the elements of formal schooling that will best meet those needs. In this view, it is altogether proper for the teacher aide to be more than a clerical aide. The usefulness of the teacher aide should be restricted only by his own personal limitations in whatever duties may be assigned to him by the regular classroom teacher.

Who Should Determine What Responsibilities Aides Should Have, What Duties They Should Perform, and What Their Responsibilities are in the Classroom and in Classroom Connected Activities?

The primary purpose of employment of teacher aides is to give legally certified teachers an opportunity to use their skills and training more efficiently and effectively. Aides should not be viewed or even considered as either substitutes or replacements for the classroom teacher. The teacher aide concept should be viewed as a separate but positive addition to the educational process. The aide is responsible to and under the direct supervision of the teacher.

The question most frequently raised is: "What tasks can and should aides be permitted to do?" To give dimension and direction to the answer to this question, action must be undertaken at two levels.

First, the faculty and local education association should determine general guidelines and policies for the employment and deployment of aides. Deployment must be contingent upon each individual's qualifications and training.

The second level of aide deployment restrictions is that of the state's legally sanctioned practices at this level.

The classroom teacher has the responsibility of being the implementator, coordinator, and director of educational programming. Moreover, it must be further recognized that the professional teacher has the added responsibility to see that students are properly evaluated, counseled, diagnosed, given individual attention when needed, in addition to attending to numerous other auxiliary duties.

The two roles of teacher and teacher-aide are separate and distinct, yet seem to cause a great deal of apprehension. The teacher is the director, the aide is the teacher's assistant. Therefore, the basic confusion would seem to be unwarranted and to be illusionary rather than a realistic threat. Educators who have not been specifically trained in personnel management are naturally somewhat reluctant to supervise aides without specific instructions. It is also understandable that initially teachers would feel more at ease with "point-at-able" instructions and duties, but later would seek to have encumbering instruction removed through implementation of their aide.

Critics tend to raise questions concerning the aide program on the point of professional adequacy or legality. However, when aide duties and functions are carefully outlined, little danger exists for "substandard teaching."

The teacher is responsible for prescribing the aide's duties and activities, the aide is directly responsible to the teacher—not to the students or to the parents. It is the teacher's responsibility to plan the classroom activities and to fit the aide in where most appropriate for ultimate student and teacher benefit.

Should There be Varying Specialties and Types of Aides? Why?

YES . . . . In order for an aide program to be effective, the personnel involved must be individually compatible with their particularly assigned task. Each resource person has certain specialties and qualities for which he is employed. Likewise, each and every aide resource person has basic limitations which should be noted and taken into consideration when deployment plans are being initiated.

> I.E. A specific aide is employed because he is indigenous to the community. It is hopeful that this move will create positive rapport between the school and the community. It would be unfair and foolhardy to assign this person to an English teacher as a theme reader.

All aide employment should be predicated on planned deployment.

Which Teachers Should be Assigned an Aide?

This must be a strictly local decision; however, there are some judgments of professional educators that should be considered when making the decisions.

Some teachers prefer to work alone and may not want aides. If this is true, the teacher should not be forced to accept an aide. Many teachers see the aide as a dilution of authority rather than an enhancement of teaching. Even though the assistance that teacher aides give to the teacher may actually increase rather than lessen her opportunity for interaction with individual children, the teacher may fear that she is losing personal contact with the children.[1]

Some teachers derive satisfaction from the performance of clerical functions. These functions are performed with ease,

---

[1] Garda W. Bowman and Gordon J. Klopf, "New Careers and Roles in the American School." A study conducted for the Office of Economic Opportunity, New York: Bank Street College of Education, September, 1967, p. 36-37, p. 153-154.

accuracy, and efficiency and often bring disproportionate rewards simply because the results are concrete.

The educational challenge is more difficult and its results are abstract. The rewards are also likely to be abstract and this leaves the less than confident professional in a somewhat uncertain position. It is understandable that these teachers are unwilling to give up their routine clerical functions and be completely exposed to the hazards of educational instruction. Although satisfaction derived from teaching in such a manner is demeaning, it is nevertheless evident.

Some teachers lack the managerial skills necessary for supervision and guidance of auxiliary personnel. An aide under this type of teacher will stagnate while an aide assisting a teacher with such managerial qualities will develop and release her potential to the benefit of the students.

A Teacher Opinion Poll taken by the NEA Research Division[2] found that 84 per cent of the teachers would like assistance with clerical duties. Although the majority of teachers seem to want aides, they do not see the employment of aides as an effective means of increasing class size nor do they think the teacher aide program should take precedence over the improvement of professional salaries in budgetary planning.

Although the majority of teachers desire teacher aides, aides should not be arbitrarily assigned. Teacher associations and unions should actively participate in the recruitment and selection of aides. Guidelines should be imposed to insure that a teacher aide will not infringe upon the professional's domain by assuming professional functions.

Personalities are vital factors that must be matched when assigning an aide to a teacher. The assignment of an aide to a

---

[2] "How the Profession Feels About Teacher Aides," *Teacher Opinion Poll, NEA Journal,* Vol. 56, No. 8, November, 1967.

teacher should be to support the teacher and the teacher must feel that her position is being supported rather than threatened by the addition of an aide to her classroom situation.

Ideally teacher aides should be assigned on a yearly basis. It is not fair to the teacher or the aide to be forced to continually readjust to new superiors or new assistants. A long term arrangement yields a situation conducive to mutual, confident, secure, relationships between teacher and aide.

The teacher must not be kept in the dark about upcoming plans concerning her. The teacher aide program concerns the teacher directly and she should be informed, included and consulted as early as possible in the formulation of plans.

What is the Teacher's Responsibility to her Assigned Aide?

Since the teacher knows exactly what her motivations are and which concepts she is developing, and since it is a common practice for the teacher and the aide to work together for the good of the children, the teacher must assume the responsibility for assisting her aide in expanding her knowledge of the children and classroom procedures. Just as it is important for a teacher to inform her aide about any special problems of a student that may be pertinent in the pupil-aide relationship, it is also important that she explain her reasons for doing certain things in certain ways.

The teacher must realize that, when the aide comes into her classroom, her teaching assignment takes on a new dimension. The teacher now has an extra set of hands, a new set of additional ideas, some new skills and a completely separate person who is interested in her work and who has a desire to help her.

When the aide comes into the classroom, a set of new relationships between teacher, aide, and students is established.

The key to a successful teacher-aide relationship is trust, flexibility and communication on the part of both the teacher and her aide.

The aide must be placed in a position that allows her to feel that she is an integral part of the classroom situation. Lesson plans and activities should include provisions for active participation of the aide in the classroom. It is the responsibility of the teacher to recognize any special talents which the aide may have and to utilize them to their fullest potential. The teacher must communicate with her aide and guide her to her ultimate achievement.

Who Should Supervise Teacher Aides?

It is difficult for a person to serve two or even three masters and while the teacher aide is an employee of the school board, the principal of the school and the teacher she is assisting, the teacher aide should be responsible to only one person: the teacher she is assisting.

The aide is in daily contact with the teacher she is assisting and performs her services directly for this teacher. Because of the nature and proximity of the aide's work, the most natural and expedient supervisor for the teacher aide is the teacher whom she is assisting.

Line supervision is easily carried out because as the aide is responsible to the teacher and the teacher is responsible to the principal, the principal is responsible to the school board.

Who Handles the Job of Dividing Classroom Responsibilities?

When a teacher takes charge of a classroom, she should naturally assume the responsibility of designating and assuming responsibilities.

In his capacity the school principal naturally assumes the traditional responsibility for supervision of the school and its entire staff. However, the teacher with a teacher aide must rely upon her own professional judgment when assuming her duties and assigning duties to her aide. The duties assigned to the aide should not infringe upon the responsibilities reserved for teachers, but only allow the aide to assist the teacher in meeting her responsibilities. Some responsibilities that are reserved for teachers specifically are the analysis of the instructional needs of the students, the prescription of educational activities to meet the students' needs and supervisory responsibilities consistent with the established school policy and directed by the school principal.

Since there are no two teachers alike, and no two aides alike, and no two teacher-aide teams alike, and most importantly, no two classroom situations alike, the assignment of aides must be left to the discretion of the teacher. The teacher must take the individual human element into consideration as she assigns teacher aide tasks.

There are several areas of duties which have been generally defined in the same terms yet can be specifically defined to demand either teacher attention or teacher aide attention. Some examples of the seemingly ambiguous terms are instruction as opposed to drill, grading and correcting papers as opposed to marking papers, and teaching a student as opposed to helping the student.

Since it has been determined that there is no universally agreed upon definition of teaching responsibilities and congruently none of teacher aides, it has become necessary to withdraw from the position that a teacher aide does not carry some instructional responsibilities. It should be emphasized, however, that the teacher has the main instructional responsibility including the responsibility for the optimum use of the aide's capabilities.[3]

How Much Planning Should be Done by the Teacher and the Teacher Aide Together?

Teachers and aide personnel need time together to plan and evaluate their work. Evaluation should be frequent, everyday, every week or when most needed and convenient to insure efficient team coordination and organization.

Cooperative evaluation and planning will enable each member of the team to better understand himself, his work and his role. The opportunity for teachers and aides to discuss problems, difficult situations and rewarding experiences, and with these things in mind, formulate plans, is essential for a successful auxiliary personnel program. To work as a team, teacher and aide must have the opportunity to plan as a team.

In some schools which are presently using teacher aides, planning sessions and individual counseling periods are a regularly scheduled part of the school day. If this is not possible, meetings could be scheduled after school hours, but compensatory factors should be taken into consideration.

Continuing and timely training of aides enhances their value to the teacher and the school in general. As the result of "on the job" training, many aides go on to qualify as full-fledged teachers.

A representative group of teachers who have worked successfully with aides in their classrooms make the following suggestions to those teachers who will be working with aides for the first time.

---

[3] *A Cooperative Study for the Better Utilization of Teacher Competencies*, Final Evaluation Report, An Evaluation Report Prepared by an Outside Evaluating Committee, Central Michigan University, Mt. Pleasant, Michigan, 1958, p. 27.

1. The teacher should get thoroughly acquainted with the aide before school begins in order to learn what the aide can do best, what her skills are, what her experiences with children have been, etc.

2. The teacher should work out beginning routines for the aide as they fit the teacher's needs, her philosophy of teaching and the aide's skills. There should be a descriptive list of aide's duties and responsibilities ready for immediate use when school begins. Revisions should be made as the need arises.

3. The teacher's schedule of time should allow for frequent, short, informal conferences with her aide as these conferences are needed.

4. Aides should be urged to take college courses in child growth and development, child psychology, methods, and other courses having relationship to the job.

5. Workshop sessions planned for aides and cooperating teachers prove valuable and should be based on needs.

6. Training sessions in the use of equipment should be provided early in the school year.

7. By attending staff meetings, local and state conferences and institutes, the aide will have an opportunity to become better acquainted with the teaching profession. This should help her to more clearly understand her role as an aide.

8. Don't hurry into the program. A few days "honeymoon" is important for orientation, with the aides spending much time observing and a little time with simple clerical tasks.

9. Teachers using aides for the first time should reorganize their thinking about instruction and plan the year's

work utilizing the aide in every possible activity to the best advantage of the students.

10. From the start, the teacher should be willing to delegate to the aide some pupil contact work such as story time, opening exercises, etc.

11. Lines of authority and relationships with other teachers, the principal, parents and the children in the room should be established at the beginning of the program.

12. The teacher must take the major responsibility for building a happy, workable secure team relationship.

13. The children in the room should be instructed as to the control authority of the aide as well as the aide's duties and responsibilities.

14. The aide should supervise students as they practice living skills—hanging up wraps, picking up after themselves, etc.

15. Both the teacher and the aide must be willing to "bend" because of their close association.

Teacher suggestions were taken from the pamphlet, "The HOW for Teachers Who Will Be Using Teacher Aides For the First Time," a Central Michigan College publication, 1958.

Specifically, on What Criteria Should the Teacher and her Aide Make Plans?

It is the responsibility of the school to develop early the supervisory talents of those teachers to whom an aide will be assigned. Ideally, a teacher-supervisor and the aide whom she will be assigned should train together at least a week before school opens and then, if feasible, should remain together.

It might well be mentioned that, while the classroom teacher sets the time for the tasks to be performed by the aide, the aide's capabilities are of prime consideration for what she can or cannot do.

Albert Einstein said, "Imagination is more important than knowledge." This should be expanded to read: "To a good teacher, imagination is more important than knowledge."

How can Supervising Teachers Help Their Aides Become More Proficient in Their Duties?

Teacher aides can become appreciably more proficient in their duties only if the local professional and employing staff realize that most of the aides training and development is their responsibility. Once they realize and accept this responsibility, planned in-service training will result and expand opportunities for aide involvement.

Aide in-service training should always be considered as an ongoing operation. Each teacher who has an aide should provide for in-service training and take into account at least the following factors:

a. Periodic and realistic face-to-face evaluation of the aides' overall school involvement.

b. Evaluation sessions with aides where they have the opportunity to discuss, to discover or identify their strengths, weaknesses, and general plans for future action.

c. Clarify reasons and means for various courses of action and activity within and without the classroom, explain why certain things are being done in certain ways and what actions or results are expected.

d. With aides, conduct tutoring or exploratory sessions designed to acquaint or to provide them with needed insights and confidence to undertake certain duties or activities.

e. Planning sessions to discuss basic student needs and ways of meeting those needs, together.

f. Workshop sessions which allow aides the opportunities to use various machines, and materials and teaches aides how to use them properly.

g. Opportunities to attend general teachers meetings in order to obtain a better perception of the concept of teachers. This will allow aides to see the teachers' gripes, their professional problems, their devotion, their interest in professional growth and their desire to provide better education in the future.

h. Have them periodically involved in community affairs.

i. Involve them in classroom connected activities that contribute to their personal growth. Provide or recomment outside reading and reference sources.

j. Encourage them to attend all system-wide aide in-service training programs that are deemed appropriate.

k. Encourage them to. participate in outside professional and personal growth courses offered by outside educational agencies either for advanced credit or for non-credit. A supervisory teacher should be aware of opportunities afforded a community by libraries, Red Cross, high school adult education courses, colleges, museums, workshops and civic centers.

How Should a Teacher Develop a Working Relationship With her Aide?

One of the first responsibilities of a teacher with a teacher aide is to get acquainted with her aide. The teacher should take the initiative in this matter, for her training and experience will enable her to make the aide a welcomed and valuable addition to her classroom.

Generally, teachers will find that aides have been selected because they possess certain qualities such as a high school education or more, a pleasant voice accented with good grammar, a neat appearance and a pleasant personality. The aide may be shy in her new surroundings, but the effective teacher can help her aide overcome this. The aide is apt to be married and have children of her own. In most instances, she will have had previous work experience and consequently knows how to take directions.

As the teacher becomes acquainted with her aide, she should inquire about her previous experience in working with groups of children. Many aides have worked with Cub Scouts, Boy Scouts, Girl Scouts, 4-H Clubs or Sunday School classes. Such a background may provide you with clues as to how your aide may be most helpful to you.

The aide's previous experiences may indicate her special interests, skills, or talents in such fields as music, art, clerical or handicraft. The teacher should know how to fit these skills into the pattern of her classroom procedure to the advantage of her students.

Probably it will be the teacher's responsibility to explain local school policies to her new helper. The aide will need to know about ethics as they apply to her new job and especially in relation to discussions she may enter into in the school or in the community. The teacher can help her aide to understand her relationship to the building staff, in faculty meetings and in connection with PTA or other school-centered community activities.

The teacher must decide specifically which duties will be assigned to her aide. Her decisions should be based on the teacher's desires coupled with her aide's abilities.

The aide's clerical services in matters of attendance, records, collections, and answer checkings will free the teacher for creative work or for work with individuals who need her special attention. By supervising students at recess or lunch or any other special times, the aide frees the teacher to prepare for other activities.

The students need to know the aide's place in matters concerning discipline. The teacher should explain the aide's position to the students and to the aide so that no unexpected problems will develop.

Training an aide should be a personal professional satisfaction to the teacher to the point where the teacher is confident of her aide's ability in any situation that the teacher may assign. At this point real team work begins.

If a teacher shares the services of an aide, she will have to take this into consideration in the planning of specific assignments and plans for her services.

A teacher with the services of an aide can look forward to a pleasant experience. The teacher will be freed from time-consuming detail and be able to devote her professional skills to improving the educational opportunities of her students.[4]

How can Teacher Aides Become a Part of an Efficient, Productive Classroom Routine?

Teacher aides can best be assimilated into the educational program through proper planning and assignment. Ideally, any conflicting individual differences held either by the teacher or the aide should be recognized and resolved before the teacher and the aide are faced with the initial classroom experience.

---

[4] Revision of the article, "The How for Teachers Who Will be Using Teacher Aides for the First Time," Central Michigan College, Mt. Pleasant, Michigan, 1958.

Individual strengths of the aide should be noted by the teacher and taken into account. Educational objectives and operational procedures should be planned in accordance with the most feasible and greatest combined strength of the teacher and the aide.

When the aide, as a third entity, enters the classroom situation, many new psychological set relationships develop between the teacher, the aide and the students. Whenever a teacher accepts a classroom aide, in any capacity, the teacher-student relationship is inevitably altered. Unless a great deal of time is spent on the many ramifications inherent in this combination, more problems will evolve from this "parlaying triangle" than from all other problem areas combined.

In-service training will satisfy many needs and resolve many problems. However, actual task orientation and indoctrination into the multifaceted educational system will primarily be the task of the teacher.

It is incumbent upon the teacher to discover and bring out any special talents the aides may have, utilizing them wisely and proficiently. It should also be incumbent upon the teacher to have not only periodic but regularly scheduled conferences devoted to guiding the aide to her fullest potential.

Surveys and experienced administrators agree that, where the direction and work assignments of the aide are concerned, there should be only one supervisor: the teacher. The success or failure of any school's endeavor rests largely with the classroom teacher, and there is no substitute for a good one.

It is important for students to understand the educational team concept. They must feel that the teacher is the educational team leader and not the "boss." The teacher who is cognizant of the fact that leadership is not command will be most successful.

It is the teacher's responsibility to set the tone of teacher-teacher aide relationships and to do so the teacher must have the full authority to make and be responsible for all classroom decisions.

Preparing teachers to train and use aides may be the best way to initiate widespread employment of auxiliary personnel in effective roles, while at the same time helping teachers overcome their reluctance and fear in accepting aides. Teachers working with nonprofessional helpers, either in or out of the classroom, must rely on their professional judgment when assigning duties to the aides.

The degree of responsibility assigned to an aide is dependent upon the interaction of the particular teacher and her particular aide, with both operating within a given structure and responding to the specific needs of the students in their particular classroom.

A delicate balance seems to be required in order to provide the specificity that yields security along with the flexibility that promotes growth. Aides must have the elasticity of personality to adapt to a myriad of school situations and policies and the teachers themselves. If a personality conflict arises, it is the teacher's responsibility to see that it does not malinger.

Aides should be assimilated into the educational team in a manner that promotes their ease, confidence, sense of belonging and pride. Creating conditions conducive to promoting these priorities in aide-classroom assimilation is the responsibility of the team leader — the teacher.

Teachers who view their aides as a positive energizing medium, allowing the teachers to increase their efficiency and effectiveness, will enjoy successful aide employment.

Gertrude Noor, reporting on a survey of teacher-aide programs undertaken for the NEA National Commission of Teacher Education and Professional Standards, said: "As they move into new ways of administering classrooms, which the aide program promotes, many teachers find renewed satisfaction in their work. They see themselves anew - imaginative, creative and able to handle anxieties which are likely to accompany change."[5]

The introduction of a teacher aide into a classroom situation provides the opportunity for close personal relationships and individual attention for students. There is a complex process of interaction between both teacher and pupils and among pupils and, through cooperative planning involving the teacher and the teacher aide, the aide can contribute to this process of interaction. However, to perform their jobs effectively, aides must have their tasks clearly defined by local school board policies in order to work with a minimum of confusion and a maximum of security.

Planning between the teacher and the aide that would promote interaction with the children might include:[6]

1. Helping the aide develop an understanding of a healthy relationship between herself, the teacher and the children.

2. Clarifying the discipline role of the aide.

3. Helping the aide recognize the need to allow children to make errors and approach tasks creatively.

4. Sharing of information between teachers and aide that will help in dealing with children.

5. Helping the aide become open-minded and objective.

---

[5] Gertrude Noor, "How Teacher Aides Feel About Their Jobs," *NEA Journal*, November, 1967, Vol. 56, No. 8.

[6] Clarence Lacny, Utilizing Teacher Aides in the Jackson, Michigan, Public Schools, "A Dual Opportunity," Jackson Public Schools, 1970.

6. Helping the aide learn how she can contribute to communications between:

   a. teacher-pupil
   b. pupil-teacher
   c. pupil-pupil

7. Helping the aide develop a realistic viewpoint about children.

8. Giving the aide a clear assignment of duties and responsibilities as they are developed.

9. Developing a team attitude.

What is to Prevent the Practice of Using Teacher Aides as a Cheaper way to Staff a Classroom?

It is understandable that violations in use of teacher aides instead of qualified teachers will be found occasionally.

Initially, the function of all auxiliary personnel in a school system should be determined and given official sanction by the appropriate agencies. The state department of education should determine the functional boundaries of those requiring only jurisdictional approval.

Basic safeguarding on the part of the local education association could easily serve as the deterrent and the policing agency for all auxiliary personnel operations.

It should be the responsibility of every teacher to see that all aides are used only in a legitimate capacity. The local educational organization should have as one of its primary responsibilities the policing of teacher aides to insure that the aides are not being exploited beyond their specified, sanctioned or certified capacities.

Should Teacher Aides be Allowed to View Student Records?

If in the performance of her duties it becomes necessary for a teacher aide to review a student's cumulative record, the aide should be allowed to do so. Not only would it be extremely difficult but also ridiculous to even attempt to set up restrictions or censorship procedures to guard against violation of confidential information.

All teacher aides regardless of their employment capacity will come into contact with certain confidential information concerning either a student or the school.

No personnel member, whether professional or nonprofessional, should be allowed to view or be given access to confidential information without prior knowledge of its restricted use and the repercussions connected with its misuse.

Any professional staff member who chooses to give confidential information to a nonprofessional is responsible for instructing the nonprofessional as to its proper use and the consequences involved in instances of its misuse.

It is imperative that the aides be made aware of the ramifications involved in their actions and the necessity of treating all confidential information with a high degree of ethical standards.

Teacher aides, when and where the necessity arises in the performance of their duties, should be allowed access to all the pertinent confidential information required. The assigned duties of an aide should specify the type and amount of personal and confidential information to be released. In fact, it should be the responsibility of the supervising teacher to see that her aide is provided with all the pertinent information needed to carry out her assigned task proficiently.

Each teacher aide, at least after her initial employment meeting, should without any doubt know that a breach of confidential ethics is inappropriate conduct for a person in her position.

High moral standards must be maintained; therefore, procedures for discipline need to be established, clarified and enforced.

Teacher aides should be allowed access to pertinent, confidential information needed in the pursuit of her duties. Often the request to view confidential records is merely a testing mechanism by which the aide checks on her position in the system. Once accorded this privilege of status, both the need and the demand for confidential information will decrease considerably.

Ethical conduct cannot be legislated, censored, restricted, controlled or enacted—it must be instilled, taught and practiced.

In What Size Schools are Teacher Aides Used Most Efficiently?

The size of the school has little direct bearing on the feasibility and implementation of the teacher aide program. The success of the teacher aide program rests on five basic factors:

1) the overall acceptance of the aide program within and without the school system

2) the means of aide employment and deployment

3) the type and quality of supervision

4) planned in-service upgrading

5) understanding of the duties to be performed and of the qualifications required at each level.

Small school systems as well as large systems can utilize teacher aides effectively. No significant difference exists between the proportion of teachers in small systems and large school systems who reported using aides (see *"How Widespread is the Use of Teacher Aides?"*). In your role as an aide, the size of the school should have little, if any, direct bearing on your tasks or proficiency. Geographically, more teachers in the West than in other regions of the country have the services of teacher aides. [7]

In the school year 1967-68, 743 school systems reported using 29,938 teacher aides. There were 2,878 aides used in kindergarten or pre-primary schools, 18,599 in elementary schools, 3,400 in junior high schools, 4,973 in senior high schools and 48 special aides or aides whose assignment was not specified.

For the school year 1968-69, there were 40,295 teacher aides employed in 799 school systems of enrollments of 6,000 or more. Of these 5,049 were in kindergarten or pre-primary schools, 25,131 in elementary schools, 3,951 in junior high schools, 4,957 in senior high schools and 1,208 were special aides or their assignments were not specified. [8]

What Features Will Make a Teacher Aide Program More Functional and Formidable?

Features that will make a teacher aide program more functional and formidable are:

1. The properly sanctioned and adopted categorical employment differences of teacher aides.

2. The creative diversity and displacement of natural talent.

---

[7] "How the Profession Feels About Teacher Aides," *Teacher Opinion Poll, NEA Journal,* Vol. 56, No. 8, November, 1967.

[8] NEA Research Bulletin, Vol. 47, No. 2, May, 1969.

3. The flexibility of aide employment.

4. The adaptability of aide deployment.

5. The development of harmonious professional and sub-professional relationships.

6. Acceptance of aides both within and without the school.

CHAPTER XI

SPECIFIC EXAMPLES OF SPECIAL AIDE USAGE

School organization is not an end in itself; it is a means of facilitating the achievement of whatever ends or purposes are deemed worthy for the school as an institution.

Henry J. Otto and David C. Sanders, *Elementary School Organization and Administration* (fourth ed.; New York: Appleton-Century and Crofts, 1964), p. 3.

It is in fact nothing short of a miracle that the modern methods of instruction have not yet entirely strangled the holy curiosity of inquiry; for this delicate little plant, aside from stimulation, stands mainly in need of freedom; without this it goes to wrack and ruin without fail.

Albert Einstein

Specific Examples of Special Aide Usage

Could Teacher Aides be "Subject or Area Specialists"?

Communities which are fortunate enough to have a person or persons with special talents or abilities, and who are willing to share these talents or abilities with students, should take advantage of the situation. The time that these people may be able to offer should be incorporated into a schedule that is flexible to benefit as many students as possible.

Such a person could "float" from class to class and school to school on a flexible schedule that would permit the aide's availability to be interwoven with the students' need and availability.

This method would allow many more students to benefit from the person's talent than is possible in the one-to-a-classroom method. This particular type of aide could also be involved in extracurricular activities during the evening hours. Rather than a scheduled class, the activity could be an informal club. A

215

strict schedule is not as important as is getting the aide and the students together when a need for the aide's presence is shown.

If these methods are not suitable, perhaps the aide could be on call. In this way, many teachers could utilize his talents at their discretion and as demanded by student needs.

Activities made feasible by such an aide should not be a part of each school day for each class. These activities would include such areas as painting, sculpting, drama, music and handicrafts.

As students mature their interests change. Older students may develop interests in specific areas such as photography or chemistry. Although a teacher may be trained to teach these subjects, there may be particular areas where a specialist would be of benefit to the students. For such areas it is possible that a local business may "lend" one of its staff members for an afternoon.

The aide should direct and guide students in areas in which the regular classroom teacher is limited, rather than assume classroom duties. Continued presence of the aide is not necessary. This particular type of aide should serve as a motivator and enhancer rather than a supervisor.

Which Specific Duties can a Counselor Aide Perform?

In November, 1966, The American Personnel and Guidance Association adopted a statement of policy encouraging the use of support personnel for the counselor. The A.P.G.A. took the position that appropriately prepared support personnel, under the supervision of the counselors, can contribute to meeting counselor's needs by enhancing the work of the counselors. [1]

---

[1] *Support Personnel for the Counselor: Their Technical and Non-Technical Roles and Preparation, Personnel and Guidance Journal,* April, 1967.

The consideration of counselor aide use and the demand for counselor aide use is an outgrowth of the social forces which are exerting pressures for increased counseling service at all levels of education.

Federal funds supporting elementary school guidance services compounded with the growing needs for this service have created a demand which is greater than our present ability to produce qualified counselors.

The assigned duties and functions of the counselor and the counselor aide are quite different and must be dealt with accordingly. The differences in the roles of the counselor and the counselor aide are reflected in their training programs. [2]

While the counselor performs a counseling function, the support personnel perform important and necessary activities that contribute to the overall service.

The support personnel performs only specific functions and only under the supervision of the counselor, while the counselor synthesizes and integrates the interrelated parts of the total range of services with and in behalf of the counselee.

The counselor performs with authoritative knowledge of effective procedures, with the use of relevant theories and with evaluation of the total procedure in mind. The aide functions with a more limited theoretical background and only in a supportive position.

Personal variations, differing local educational philosophy and objectives and local working conditions make it difficult to standardize preparation of counselor aides. However, the A.P.G.A. supports its concept that two years of structured graduate work is desirable for all school counselors.

---

[2] Ibid., p. 859.

217

Even the three traditional counselor preparation activities (1. formal classroom didactic instruction, 2. practical and in-service education, and 3. on-the-job training) vary in emphasis when used in training counselor aides. Emphasis is placed on the development of skills, rather than understanding, with the presumption that learning will be best accomplished in an on-the-job setting. Under these circumstances, close supervision is essential. [3]

The duties of an aide are divided into two groups: those of direct helping relationships and those of indirect helping relationships. [4]

Direct helping relationships are those activities which relate to both individual and small-group interviewing functions which the counselor feels the aide may adequately do.

Indirect helping relationships are such as information gathering and processing, assisting with referrals, placement and follow-up procedures and program management. Clerical duties are included in this category but they should not be stressed. If the job description is mainly clerical then it would be better to hire a secretary and give some counselor aide training.

A good counselor aide training program should have at least four major phases: 1) screening and admission, 2) preservice orientation to the job, 3) in-service preparation, and 4) on-the-job training. [5]

---

[3] James W. Costar, "Training Programs for School Counselor Aides," Department of Counseling, Personnel Services and Educational Psychology, Michigan State University, East Lansing, Michigan, 1970.

[4] *Support Personnel for the Counselor: Their Technical and Non-Technical Roles and Preparation*, op. cit.

[5] Costar, op. cit.

It is imperative that the aide be oriented to the nature of the human learning process, the school in which he assists, and the nature of his job well enough to begin work skillfully. These personal characteristics are usually acquired through didactic experiences in courses or workshops conducted during the summer.

It should be expected that an aide will continue to develop his skill and understanding through participation in a continuous in-service training program. On-the-job training may be the most important part of the training of a counselor aide because an aide is judged upon the skill he exhibits in performance and because this skill is developed in performance, constant close supervision is important.

It is also evident that the aide's training should include experiences which increase his ability to accept and give supervision for eventually the aide will find himself actively participating in the training of new aides.[6]

Which Specific Duties can a Library Aide Perform?

The library aide performs technical tasks of a nonprofessional nature under the direction of a professional librarian or other supervisor. These tasks could include assisting students in gathering materials for reports, doing library research for the teachers, keeping the library cards and records in order, helping to develop supplementary book and magazine lists and helping the librarian select books for the library.

The aide would not perform tasks which require a professional knowledge of librarianship, but would do such tasks as clerical

---

[6] Ibid.

functions. The aide could perform technical tasks such as paging and circulating books, filing and typing, preparation and upkeep of library materials, maintenance of shelves, files and equipment, record keeping, cataloging and minor informational services such as answering directional questions about the use of basic reference tools.

The library aide could be training in a terminal program offered by a local community college or in an in-service training program handled by the supervising librarian.

The college curriculum should include general education courses, library technical courses and related business and office courses. [7]

General education courses would include communication skills, English composition, social sciences, humanities and physical sciences.

Library technical courses would include an introduction to libraries and library operation, circulation and information, media production and equipment handling and practical experience and supervised field work.

Business and office skills would include typing, business math, office machines, data processing, office management and operation of equipment and tools used in preparation and circulation of library materials.

In-service training by the supervising librarian would not include the general education courses but would include library technical skills and business and office skills as required by the needs of the particular library in which the aide will be employed.

---

[7] *Draft of Guidelines for Training Programs for Library Technical Assistants,* Library Education Division, American Library Association, 50 E. Huron Street, Chicago, Illinois, April, 1968.

Basic in-service training should include instruction in the Dewey Decimal System of shelving books and the location of various types of reference materials. The aide should also be trained to setup and maintain a charge tray for materials circulated, store magazines, use the card catalogue and Reader's Guide to Periodicals, inventory library materials and set up an attractive display.

Which Specific Duties can a Physical Education Aide Perform?

The increased size of physical education classes has resulted in little more than supervised mass recreation hours rather than physical education for the school children. In many schools, physical education teachers are not available and the responsibility for physical education, hygiene, recreation and sportsmanship falls on the teachers. Teachers who are not prepared to lead a class in physical activity are likely to cover their eyes and pray for the end of the hour.

Physical education aides can give physical education teachers more time to teach by taking care of routine chores such as attendance, giving written and skill tests, keeping records and charting progress, developing and preparing audio-visual aides, maintaining and dispersing equipment, and policing locker rooms. Physical education aides can also be insurance that students in schools without specific physical education teachers are given some meaningful physical education.

The aide is often able to take charge of a small group for instruction while the teacher works with the larger group or the aide may supervise the larger group while the teacher gives individualized instruction. Aides can also serve as demonstrators and safety spotters when the class is using equipment that needs added supervision such as a trampoline.

An aide may be particularly skillful in one area and be able to teach skills to the class which the teacher cannot, thereby adding to the range of classroom exposure. It is possible to have an area specialist such as a first aide instructor or nutritionist who can give the students more complete instruction than the teacher could.

First aide instructors are trained and certified by the American Red Cross. Such aides can give students knowledge that can save many lives.

The Red Cross also trains and certifies Water Safety Instructors. These aides could teach students to swim and in so doing, insure their safety in water activities in and out of school.

In Covina Valley, California, where physical education teachers are available, an attempt is made to schedule at least one aide to each physical education teacher for each class period. [8] To give continuity to the program and develop sound teacher-teacher aide relationships aides are requested to work at least two consecutive class hours.

Many of the Covina aides are college students and are not able to work a full school day, so the schools are likely to have two or three different aides per day. In this way the college students are getting practical classroom experience and the schools are better staffed.

In the Covina district the aides have a starting wage of $1.82 per hour. The average wage is $2.00 per hour.

Initially, the aides were sought in the college athletic departments and student placement bureaus, with special emphasis

---

[8] *How Aides Can Improve a Physical Education Program, School Management,* January, 1957, p. 57-8.

on potential physical education teachers. As the idea was publicized, housewives and other students volunteered for the program yielding an abundance of aides. Potential physical education aides should have some training in physical education-type activities and have had experience in handling large groups.

A study of the Covina program indicated that when relieved of supervisory and store-keeping duties, the physical education teachers had up to 45 per cent more time for actual instruction and individual attention in physical educational activities.

What Specific Duties can a Special Education Aide Perform?

Aides in special education classrooms can perform clerical functions such as maintaining attendance records; maintaining and filing general organizational records; preparing, distributing and maintaining classroom materials and equipment.

Aides can help teachers to better meet the needs of these special students by making observations and reporting to the teacher in charge. Aides may also administer routine tests and report to the teacher or chart each student's progress.

Although the teacher should be completely responsible for preparing the lesson plan, the aide can take an active part in presenting a part of the plan to the students.

The aide is especially helpful in this matter for she allows for double adult-pupil contact and can double the teacher's perception of students and their individual problems. In this function the aide is performing her primary task, that of extending the human emotional responsivity of the professional person. [9]

---

[9] Field Testing and Demonstration of On-The-Job Training of Paraprofessionals to Serve as Members of Teams Operating Type-A Classrooms for Mentally Handicapped, Accompanied by In-Service Training of Teachers Serving on Teams, Branch County Intermediate School Offices, 66 S. Monroe Street, Coldwater, Michigan, p. 19.

In performing this function, the aide is oriented toward three objectives: [10]

1. Helping handicapped children attain their highest achievement level by concentrating on what the student can do well and praising him for it. The addition of an aide to a classroom will allow more personal adult contact for the student by both the teacher and the aide. Both adults will then have more time to motivate and encourage students.

2. Helping handicapped children to build a better self-concept. Handicapped children are faced not only with coping with their limitations but also the complications of non-sympathetic and overly-sympathetic people in the outside world. Handicapped children need help in accepting and valuing themselves.

3. Helping the handicapped child develop the curiosity which is a sign of the person who has developed enough self-confidence to leave his sheltered, sure surroundings and explore. The handicapped child must have encouragement to develop interpersonal relationships. The aide can be a party to one of these initial relationships that will assist the handicapped child in developing confidence.

[10] Ibid., p. 20.

APPENDIX

THE M.S.U. EFFORT—A BRIEF LOOK

The volunteer effort began at Michigan State University with the Student Education Corps in 1962. The S.E.C. has become the largest of the volunteer programs at M.S.U. as well as the largest student-operated volunteer program in the United States with an annual involvement of close to 1,500 students.

The S.E.C. was followed by the Campus Community Commission in 1964, the S.T.E.P. Project (Student Education Project) in 1965, and the S.C.O.P.E. Project (Students for Community Organization Through Panhellenic Effort) in 1966. Since 1966, the expansion and growth of this area is tremendous. Rather than trace each new program or project, an attempt will be made to highlight the current variety of activity.

Student Education Corps: Working in 72 schools in Lansing and other cities at all levels (Head Start through adult education and including special education). Volunteers provide individual tutoring and teacher assistance during school hours.

Campus Community Commission: Operating on the north side of Lansing, this program is run by a coalition of teenagers and college students. It offers after school, evening, and Saturday activities for over 400 children. The activities include tutoring, arts and crafts, educational games, outings, camp trips, and recreation. For adults, classes are held in a variety of subjects including a class for high school drop-outs who wish to take the G.E.D. exam for high school quality.

Student Education Project: This summer program works at Rust College, Holly Springs, Mississippi, manning a summer study skills institute for incoming freshmen. All Rust College freshmen participate in the 5-week institute which is run entirely by volunteers.

Students for Community Organization Through Panhellenic Effort: A project of Panhellenic Council, involves the manning of a community center by college students and aiding in the activities of that center.

Other programs: Volunteers working at the Lansing Job Training Center with remedial classes as well as technical skills groups and individual counseling. Preschool programming at home with volunteers running work and play groups for ages two and three. Junior Achievement volunteers working as company advisors, graduate students offering tutoring, study halls, and counseling for incoming freshmen from minority groups. Budget planning and home economic classes. Staffing and Reading Room for the Blind at the library. Fine Arts clubs and classes at neighborhood action centers taught by volunteers. Group counseling and classes for inmates at Michigan Training Unit, Ionia. A Big-Brother and Big-Sister program for children and teenagers from Lansing. A variety of activities for volunteers who work at the Michigan School for the Blind. A college center program where volunteers man an information and study-tutor center for inner-city youth interested in further education. Ham radio and commercial radio clubs at action centers. Student Volunteers helped man the Lansing Rumor Control Center. Recreation and arts and crafts program at Turn-Key housing project.

M.S.U. VOLUNTEER PHILOSOPHY

There is no single philosophy behind the volunteer effort at Michigan State University, but rather a series of philosophies developed over time. The current collection of principles serve not only as a justification for Michigan State University's involvement in the area, but also as a basis of operation for the area.

One of the most important tenants of the volunteer movement is that government and industry alone cannot solve all the social problems facing our nation. The interest and work of the individual citizen on a voluntary basis is an equally effective force. It is our hope that through involving students in meaningful volunteer programs during college, they may gain additional insights into the effectiveness of individual citizen effort. Today's problems are everyone's problems, each man has a role to play in their solution.

The growth of volunteer programs is a further extension of the Land Grant philosophy of practical education and service to the people of the state. Volunteer programs often provide practical firsthand experiences in which the lessons of the classroom can be tested and reinforced. This inherent educational value is present in most of the volunteer activities students engage in. The other essential element in the Land Grant philosophy is service to the people of the state. This university has a proud tradition of service by its faculty and staff. Service by students is a realistic extension of this tradition.

Beyond these overall philosophies, four specific objectives for the volunteer effort have been identified. The most important of these is our commitment to student-run programs. Most of our successful programs have been built around the student-run model. Basically, a student-run program is one in which students are involved in decision making, recruiting volunteers, arranging facilities, fund-raising, evaluation, and all other aspects which effect programming. This type of a model is desirable for two reasons. First is the opportunity this model provides for student leadership and initiative. Second, is the success students have in recruiting their peers. It would be easy for us to just place students with a particular agency in Lansing, but this practice gives the student no sense of real commitment or an opportunity to make his opinions and ideas count. Realistically, there are a number of drawbacks to the student-run model, such as continuity of programming, dependability, etc., but these can be dealt with by providing overall coordination through the Office of Volunteer Programs and advisement from faculty, staff and this office.

A second objective is to develop programs which will be geared to the academic pursuits and interests of the students. This means involving business administration students in a program like Junior Achievement, or education majors in the Student Education Corps, etc.. If the volunteer programs are to provide useful, meaningful service to the community, specific skills and abilities must be found. In order to interest students, volunteer programs must provide opportunities for the use of their particular talents and educational backgrounds.

A third objective is to provide programs which vary in level of commitment. We fully realize that different students will have different commitments in this area. Student commitment will vary in time given, reason for involvement, duration of involvement, and type of involvement. There are needs within the community for all levels of commitment. The duty of volunteer programs is to match student commitment with appropriate opportunities within the community. One additional point should be stressed. Experience has shown that level of commitment usually goes up when the volunteer sees a need firsthand and becomes a part of filling that need.

The fourth objective of the volunteer effort is to make students more relevant. During the past several years, the university has been criticized by students for its lack of relevance. No doubt some of this citicism was deserved, but the responsibility for relevancy within the university must be assumed by students as well. One way students can become more relevant is through volunteer community action projects. If students become relevant, their classes will be more relevant as well.

These, then, are the principles under which M.S.U. volunteer programs operate, the philosophy which motivates the program, and the call to action which volunteer programs seek to answer.

THE OFFICE OF VOLUNTEER PROGRAMS

The Office of Volunteer Programs at Michigan State University was established in November of 1967 by the Board of Trustees to provide additional support for volunteer service efforts. Operating under the Vice President for Student Affairs, the office attempts to provide that support through a variety of activities and services.

One of the major roles the Office of Volunteer Programs assumes is the establishment and maintenance of programs. The office represents the university for the volunteer program area in dealing with community agencies, organization, and groups. Especially in the initiating of new programs, this role is an important one. In order to satisfy actual community identified needs *while* providing meaningful experiences for volunteers, the design and implementation of programs requires careful consideration and planning. Too often programs are designed to meet only one condition (either satisfying needs or providing experiences). These programs usually suffer from lack of participation by community residents or by volunteers. Therefore, in the initiating function, the Office of Volunteer Programs attempts to build both conditions into programs. In addition, volunteers usually would rather work with people than with things. We attempt to provide these kinds of experiences. In working with the setup of student programs, we stress the difference between long-term programs versus short-term or one-shot projects. The problems inherent in long-term programs such as continuity, sustaining a program after the initial "new and exciting" stage, or financing, etc., are presented by the Volunteer Programs staff so that a student or student group may carefully evaluate their program plans. After the type of program is determined (long-term, short-term, or one-shot), we aid the students in drawing up a proposed program. After a possible program plan is developed, the Volunteer Programs Office arranges meetings between community representatives and student representatives. It is out of these sessions that the final program is established. Much the same procedure is followed when a community agency, organization, or group contacts the Office of Volunteer Programs desiring to set up a program. Of course, there are other aspects of the initiating function but the particulars are not necessary to this overview.

The Office of Volunteer Programs also has a responsibility for overall co-ordination of the volunteer service efforts. Co-ordinating volunteer programs avoids duplication of effort as well as promoting cooperation between volunteer programs. There is also a need to co-ordinate volunteer programs with other community programs and university programs. Co-operation between volunteer programs and non-voluntary programs is reinforcing and necessary. The leadership of the various M.S.U. volunteer programs meets together to see what they can work on as a group. This cooperative effort includes fund raising, recruiting, common services, volunteer training, support of new groups, and, to a great extent, the advising of the Office of Volunteer Programs. Likewise, the Office of Volunteer Programs assumes the supervision of the joint efforts. Three results of these joint efforts will be presented later in this section.

An additional role played by the Office of Volunteer Programs is the advisement of programs. This advisement is done in the initiating of all programs and continues for programs which are all-university in nature, drawing upon several disciplines, or groups for their volunteers. In specific programs centering around specific interest groups or disciplines, the advisement function is almost solely in terms of consultation.

A growing number of services are offered through the Volunteer Programs Office. The office provides technical assistance to programs on other campuses. Since the M.S.U. Office of Volunteer Programs is the only venture of its kind at a college or university, this service is used frequently. The office provides technical assistance to several Lansing groups and agencies on voluntary program efforts. The office provides secretarial assistance as well as mimeograph and other duplicating services for volunteer programs. It also provides a limited amount of office space, telephone service, etc., for a number of volunteer programs. In addition, a small resource library and materials center is operated for the programs.

Other services are offered through the cooperation of all volunteer programs through the Office of Volunteer Programs. These include joint on-campus and off-campus fund raising, a general recruitment drive, and the development of an overall *M.S.U. Volunteer* program. All students serving as volunteers in any program are M.S.U. volunteers. Each carries an M.S.U. Volunteer card and receives a monthly newsletter, *Volunteer Viewpoint*. M.S.U. Volunteers also are invited to take part in special activities, workshops, and seminars planned by the Volunteer Programs Office. There is a much more important reason for the M.S.U. Volunteer program. Its purpose is to develop a sense of oneness among all volunteers who, no matter what they are doing, have in common an interest in voluntary action to promote social change and improvement.

Two major services of the Office of Volunteer Programs are the M.S.U. Volunteer Bureau and the Volunteer Transportation Pool.

M.S.U. VOLUNTEER BUREAU

The M.S.U. Volunteer Bureau serves as a central information and recruitment center for the various M.S.U. volunteer programs as well as many community agencies, organizations and groups. The Bureau is designed to serve individuals who desire to work as volunteers. Operating as a branch of the Office of Volunteer Programs, the Bureau will work with individuals while the Volunteer Programs Office will work with groups.

The Bureau solves several problems. Students often had to seek out five or six agencies in order to be placed as a volunteer. On the other hand, many Lansing agencies complained that students called several agencies for a placement. Each agency eventually arranged a placement for the student with only one student to fill as many as four different placements from four different agencies. The student can now seek a volunteer placement at the M.S.U. Volunteer Bureau and find out about all opportunities available with either an M.S.U. volunteer program or a Lansing agency. Because of the obvious benefits to them, many Lansing agencies will only accept students who are placed through the M.S.U. Volunteer Bureau.

The M.S.U. Volunteer Bureau works closely with the Lansing Central Volunteer Bureau of the Community Services Council. The Bureau also has information application, etc., for VISTA, Teacher Corps, Upward Bound, and other federal programs using volunteers, paid and unpaid. Information is also available on other volunteer programs across the country needing volunteers such as the American Red Cross, the American Friends Service, or the National Service Secretariat.

VOLUNTEER TRANSPORTATION POOL

One of the early realities faced by student volunteer programs was the need for adequate transportation to get to points within the community where student volunteers were needed. The Volunteer Transportation Pool solves this problem.

The pool is equipped with ten vehicles. Six 12-passenger vans and four 6-passenger sedans. In addition the pool employs drivers for the vehicles. The pool is available for use by all M.S.U. volunteer programs through the Office of Volunteer Programs.

GLOSSARY

This glossary contains the author's interpretation of terms as applied to this text.

ACADEMIC — conforming to formalized scholastic functions, traditions and rules

ACADEMIC FREEDOM — that freedom which is granted to educators to teach their personal convictions and also that freedom allowing students to learn, inquire, or challenge in any field of exploration without fear of obstruction, dismissal, harassment or other reprisal

ACT-OUT — direct observable expression of feelings, usually hostile or aggressive feelings aimed at supervision or authority

ACT-UP — direct, observable expression of hostile or otherwise undesirable behavior

ADMINISTRATION — the physical process of attending to the function and operation of an institution

ADMINISTRATORS — those who are responsible for the structure and function of the school and its programs

ADULT OUT-REACH PROGRAM — school-related programs which are designed to bring the adult into the school community

ANCILLARY — referring to subordinate personnel employed to assist the professional with non-instructional duties

ANIMOSITY — expressed feelings of resentment or hostility

ARBITRARILY ASSIGNED — assignment of personnel made by the administrators with consideration of personality and ideological factors of personnel involved

AUDIO-VISUAL AIDS — material with sound and/or sight stimulus

AUXILIARY PERSONNEL — personnel employed to assist the professional in performing her duties

CAPACITY — limits of ability or responsibility

CATEGORICAL — in the form of a category

CATEGORY — division formed for the purpose of a given discussion or classification

CERTIFICATION	a statement by an official body which gives credibility to a person or institution which has met certain prescribed standards
CERTIFIED AIDE	an aide who has been certified by the state in which she is employed
CLASSIFICATION	grouping by similarities of subject, employment, etc., as systematic arrangement of job titles by responsibilities
CLASSLOAD	number of students in a classroom
CLASSROOM CHALLENGE	the task of meeting student needs
CLASSROOM ROUTINE	daily procedure developed in the individual classroom
COGNIZANT	awareness of the properties and relationships of an object
COMMENSURATE	equal to, corresponding in size, amount, degree of nature
COMMUNICATION GAP	the difference between what one person says and how another interprets it
COMMUNITY	a group of people living in the same locality or a given area unified by a common bond
COMMUNITY MORES	fixed local customs which have the force of law
COMPULSORY OBLIGATION	responsibility that must be fulfilled or the person responsible will be faced with reprimand
CONDUCIVE	helpful, contributive, encouraging environment
CONFIDENTIAL	private, not for general knowledge
CONSEQUENTIAL INFORMATION	information logically related so that the former validates the latter
CONTEMPORARY	at this time, current practice
CONTRIBUTION	the giving of ideas, assistance and/or moral support
CREATIVITY	ability to produce a work of thought or imagination, particularly art
CRITERIA	a test by which anything is evaluated in forming a pure and correct judgment respecting it

CRITERION	an evaluative standard on which a decision or judgment may be based
CULTURAL	pertaining to the knowledge, belief, art, morals, or customs and habits acquired by man as a member of his society
DEFICIENCIES	lack of normal development in intelligence or a lack of specified curriculum in the classroom
DEPLOYMENT	means of implementing employment for a specific task assignment
DIAGNOSTICIAN	one trained in identifying deficiencies from symptoms presented
DIFFERENTIATED ROLES	distinguishing behavior which is proper for each specific role
DIMENSION	scope or importance
DISCIPLINE	the inhibition of behavior
ECONOMIC FACTORS	sociological term describing the effect of income on environment
EDUCATIONAL PROCESS	the act of changing behavior, teaching students the desired information
EDUCATIONAL PURIST	one who believes in the traditional views of education
EFFICIENT	employment of the most acceptable means for the most productive ends
EMPLOYMENT	serving in a particular capacity with the purpose of financial gain
ENRICHMENT	to improve or to make more meaningful the means and matter of instruction
ENTITY	a distinct unit
ENVIRONMENT	external conditions and influences which affect the life and development of an organism
ENVIRONMENTAL CONDITIONING	knowledge acquired within the environment for acting in accordance with the behavior standards within the environment
EXEMPLARY	serving as an illustration or guide, generally that which is considered to be of the best

235

FEASIBILITY	practicality, capability of being completed successfully
FLOATER	an aide who moves from class to class and school to school as needed
FRINGE BENEFITS	benefits generally considered other than monetary, not of primary concern
GRADED SYSTEM	school systems using a class or grade-line division normally representing the work of one academic year, this term can be applied to either the students or to the tasks appropriate to a given year, a means of denoting student placement standing in the kindergarten through grade 12
IMPLEMENT	activate, put into effect
INCONSEQUENTIAL INFORMATION	information which is not meaningful to the particular subject
INCUMBENT	an obligatory act, imposed as a duty, responsibility or obligation
INDIGENOUS	quality gained from having lived in an area or community for an extended period of time
INDIGENT	in need of financial assistance
INDIVIDUALIZED INSTRUCTION	instruction designed to meet the needs of each individual student
INDOCTRINATE	to instruct in the rudiments or principles
INDUCEMENT	a persuasive element enticing one to behave in a particular manner
INGENUITY	inventiveness, cleverness, creativity
INHERENT	a permanent and unchangeable form existing in a person or object
INITIAL OUTLAY	the first expenditure of money or effort
INITIATE	to begin or start, to facilitate the first action
INITIATIVE	quality of drive and enthusiasm for beginning and carrying through projects
INNOVATIVE	a quality of being creative
INNOVATION	a new idea or practice

INNOVATORS	those who initiate new ideas and practices
INSTRUCTIONAL	giving new knowledge and direction
INTERNSHIP	period during which a student teacher would teach under the direct supervision of a certified teacher
JUSTIFICATION	the process of proving need or desirability of an act
LEGAL SANCTION	authority and credence given by law
MATRIARCHAL DOMINATION	overbundance of female authority
MATRICULATE	become a regularly enrolled member of the student body
MEDIATOR	one who acts to bring two conflicting persons together, usually by compromise
MONITOR	to watch an activity or operation and give warning when malfunction occurs
NEBULOUS	vague, without concrete grounds
NON-GRADED SYSTEM	a school system without the divisions which normally represent the work of the school year
NONINSTRUCTIONAL	duties which are concerned with essential but non-teaching qualities
NONPROFESSIONAL	duties which are not instructional or administrative
NON-TEACHING DUTIES	auxiliary, supportive duties
ORDERED	concrete structure with specific procedures
ORIENTATION	period during which you become accustomed to a new situation
PATRIARCHAL DOMINATION	situation in which the male is the authority figure
PERFUNCTORY OBLIGATIONS	routine duties
PHILOSOPHIES	a way of looking at and acting about an idea
PLACEMENT	arrangement or assignment
POTENTIAL	degree of ability not yet utilized

PREVENTIVE EDUCATIONAL MEASURES	measures aimed at preventing rather than remedying educational errors
PRIMARY AIM	the goal with which you are most concerned attaining
PROFESSIONAL	concerned with instructional or administrative duties
PROFESSIONAL DISTANCE	not becoming attached to or assimilated into a work or peer group below your professional status
PROFICIENT	able to do a job well
PSYCHOLOGICAL SET	a person's psychological make-up which causes him to act or react in a certain manner
PURISTS	those opposed to the introduction of new procedures and practices
RAMIFICATIONS	adverse reactions to an action
RAPPORT	a relationship in which there is understanding and free communication and expression
RATIONALIZATION	process by which one justifies actions, an ego-defensive method
REALISTICALLY	giving truths factually
REMEDIAL EDUCATION	education directed toward the student with limited abilities
SAMPLING	a representative group of the whole
SCAPEGOAT	person used for the displacement of guilt or aggression
SCHOOL POLICY	procedure for handling situations usually not deviated from
SCHOOL PROCEDURE	method of channeling information, requests and instruction
SECONDARY AIM	the second most important goal
SESSIONS	periods of time, usually relating to specific subjects such as orientation sessions
SIBLING	brothers and sisters of a particular child
SIGNIFICANT DIFFERENCE	credible element with substantial differential evidence

SIGNIFICANT FACTOR	an element which is credible and has substantial evidence
SIMULATION	a copy or act containing similarities but not the real thing
SOCIAL ENVIRONMENT	the surroundings, especially people, in which a person lives
SPORADICALLY SPACED	placed at random, not specifically or visibly ordered
STATUTES	a law declared by the legislature
STEREOTYPING	classing all people in one group and thereby giving them all the qualities of the group because they have one quality of that group
STIMULI	plural of "stimulus"
STIMULUS	a motivating or energizing factor
STRUCTURED	given shape, order and form
STUDENT IN-REACH PROGRAM	program designed to encourage and assist students in school
SUPERFICIAL	irrelevant and immaterial, not meaningful
SUPERVISING TEACHER	the professional teacher in charge of the classroom
TEACHER-TEACHER AIDE TEAM	cooperative work structure of a professional and a non-professional auxiliary
TEACHER TURNOVER	rate at which teachers leave a school system and must be replaced
TEACHING DUTIES	instructional tasks for which the teacher is responsible
TECHNOLOGY	applied science
TERMINOLOGY	choice and use of words
THEORETICAL	practice or belief supported by theory
THEORY	a general principle supported by considerable data
TRIVIA	insignificant material
TUTOR	the person in charge of the tutorial conference

TUTORIAL CONFERENCE   act of giving assistance to an individual or a small group

VINDICATE   free from any question of guilt or negligence

BIBLIOGRAPHY

Alexander, S. Kern, "What Teacher Aides Can-And Cannot-Do," *Nations Schools*, Vol. 82, No. 2, August, 1968.

Anderson, Robert H., *Teaching in a World of Change*, New York: Harcourt, Brace and World, 1966, Chapter 6, "The People Who Work with Teachers," p. 7.

Bain, Winifred E.

Baruch, Bernard

Boudreau, Sister Phyllis, C.N.D., "Teacher Aides," *NCEA Bulletin*, August, 1967.

Bowman, Garda W., and Klopf, Gordon J., *Auxiliary School Personnel: Their Roles, Training, and Institutionalization*. A study conducted for the Office of Economic Opportunity, New York: Bank Street College of Education, October, 1966.

Bowman, Garda W., and Klopf, Gordon J., "New Careers and Roles in the American School." A study conducted for the Office of Economic Opportunity, New York: Bank Street College of Education, September, 1967, p. 36-37, p. 153-154.

Branick, John J., "How to Train and Use Teacher Aides," *Phi Delta Kappan*, October, 1966, Vol. XLVIII, No. 2.

Bruner, Jerome S., *The Process of Education*, Cambridge, Mass.: Harvard University Press, 1962, p. 1.

Clemet, Stanley L., "Staffing for Better Schools," U.S. Department of Health, Education and Welfare, U.S. Government Printing Office, Division of Printing, Washington, D.C., 1967, p. 14.

Costar, James W., "Training Programs for School Counselor Aides," Department of Counseling, Personnel Services and Educational Psychology, Michigan State University, East Lansing, Michigan, 1970.

Cutler, Marilyn H., "Teacher Aides Are Worth the Effort," *Nation's Schools*, April, 1964, p. 67-69, p. 116-118.

Dawson, Mary, *Elementary School Organization*, Washington, D.C.: *National Elementary Principal*, 1961, p. 4.

Einstein, Albert

Ellis, Patricia and Meyer, Dorothy V., "The Teacher Evaluates Innovations," *NEA Journal*, December, 1967.

Frank, Lawrence K., in Association for Supervision and Curriculum Development, *New Insights and the Curriculum*, Washington, D.C.: The Association, 1963, p. 18.

Glovinsky, Dr. Arnold and Johns, Dr. Joseph P., "A Quiz for Educators," *Nation's Schools*, Vol. 82, No. 2, August, 1968, p. 24.

Goldstein, David H., Executive Director of the Indianapolis Preschool Center, Inc., Indiana, *The Instructor*, October, 1966.

241

Hockett, John A. & Jacobson, E. W., *Modern Practices in Elementary School,* ed., Boston, Ginn, 1943, p. 125.

Janowitz, Gayle, *Helping Hands,* University of Chicago Press, Chicago, Illinois, 1965.

Lacny, Clarence, Utilizing Teacher Aides in the Jackson, Michigan, Public Schools, "A Dual Opportunity," Jackson Public Schools, 1970.

Lieberman, Myron, *The Future of Public Education,* Phoenix Books, The University of Chicago Press, Chicago, Illinois, 1967, p. 100.

Malvesta, Daniel and Ronayne, Eugene L., "Cops in the Classroom," *NEA Journal,* December, 1967.

Mann, Horace

McMurrin, Sterling M., edited by, "How We Drive Teachers to Quit," by Richard Meryman, from *Student, School and Society,* 1964, p. 237.

Miller, Richard I., *Education in a Changing Society,* Washington, D.C.: National Education Association, 1963, p. 9.

Neubauer, Dorothy, *Contemporary Society: Background for the Instructional Program,* Washington, D.C.: National Education Association, 1957, p. 7.

Noor, Gertrude, "How Teacher Aides Feel About Their Jobs," *NEA Journal,* November, 1967, Vol. 56, No. 8.

Otto, Henry J. & Sanders, David C., *Elementary School Organization and Administration,* Fourth Edition, New York: Appleton-Century-Crofts, 1964, p. 3.

Reissman, Frank and Pearl, Arthur, *New Careers for the Poor,* New York: Free Press, 1965.

Rioux, William J., "Here Are Fourteen Ways to Use Nonteachers in Your School District," *Nation's Schools,* December, 1965.

Rioux, William J., "At The Teacher's Right Hand," *American Education,* December, 1965-January, 1966, p. 5-6.

Stephens, John M., *The Psychology of Classroom Learning,* New York: Holt, Rinehart and Winston, Inc., 1965, p. 9.

Thomson, Scott D., *The Emerging Role of the Teacher Aide,* The Clearing House, February, 1963, p. 326-30.

Wilcox, Betty, "What is the Teacher Aide's Role," *Minnesota Journal of Education,* May, 1967.

PUBLIC DOCUMENTS AND REPORTS

A Look at Teacher Aides and Their Training, Metropolitan Educational Research Association, Michigan State University, East Lansing, Michigan, 1968.

Auxiliary School Personnel, National Commission on Teacher Education and Professional Standards, National Education Association, 1967.

Auxiliary School Personnel: Their Roles, Training and Institutionalization, based on a nation-wide study conducted for the U.S. Office of Economic Opportunity, Bank Street College of Education, New York, October, 1966.

A Cooperative Study for the Better Utilization of Teacher Competencies, Final Evaluation Report, An Evaluation Report Prepared by an Outside Evaluating Committee, Central Michigan University, Mt. Pleasant, Michigan, 1958, p. 27.

Development of Teacher Aide Programs, U.S. Congressional Record, Vol. 113, Washington, D.C., January 30, 1968, No. 12.

Draft of Guidelines for Training Programs for Library Technical Assistants, Library Education Division, American Library Association, 50 E. Huron Street, Chicago, Illinois, April, 1968.

Education Profession Act, P.L. 90-35 Sec. 520, Title V, Part B., Higher Education Act of 1965, amended.

Field Testing and Demonstration of On-The-Job Training of Paraprofessionals to Serve as Members of Teams Operating Type-A Classrooms for Mentally Handicapped, Accompanied by In-Service Training of Teachers Serving on Teams, Branch County Intermediate School Offices, 66 S. Monroe Street, Coldwater, Michigan, p.19.

Education Research Service Circular No. 2, April, 1967, p. 9.

Estimates of School Statistics, 1967-68, National Education Association Research Report.

Ford Foundation: Fund for the Advancement of Education, A Report for 1952-54, New York, Ford Foundation, 1954, p. 28.

Guide for Preparing a State Plan for Attracting and Qualifying Teachers to Meet Critical Teacher Shortages, Part B, subpart 2, of the Education Professions Development Act (Title V of the Higher Education Act of 1965).

Guidelines for Special Programs for Educationally Deprived Children, Department of Health, Education and Welfare, Office of Education, Draft, October 5, 1965, p. 20.

How Aides Can Improve a Physical Education Program, School Management, January, 1957, p. 57-58.

"How the Profession Feels About Teacher Aides," *Teacher Opinion Poll,* NEA Journal, Vol. 56, No. 8, November, 1967.

Kentucky, O.A.C., No. 269-1963.

MSU Volunteer, A Handbook on Volunteer Programs for Faculty and Staff, Office of Volunteer Programs, 101 Student Services Building, Michigan State University, East Lansing, Michigan, 1969.

243

The National School Volunteer Program, Public Education Association, 24 W. 40th Street, New York, New York.

Paraprofessionalism in the Schools of Wayne County, Michigan, Report of the Paraprofessional Study, ESEA Title III, Wayne County Intermediate School District, Detroit, Michigan, September, 1968, p. 16-17.

The Practice and the Promise, Paraprofessionalism in the Schools of Wayne County, Michigan, Report of the Paraprofessional Study, ESEA Title IV, Wayne County Intermediate School District, Detroit, Michigan, September, 1968.

A *Revision of a Cooperative Study for the Better Utilization of Teacher Competencies*, Final Evaluation Report, an Evaluation Report Prepared by an Outside Evaluating Committee, Central Michigan University, Mt. Pleasant, Michigan, 1958.

Revision of the article, "The How for Teachers Who Will Be Using Teacher Aides for the First Time," Central Michigan College, Mt. Pleasant, Michigan, 1958.

Staffing for Better Schools, Office of Education, U.S. Department of Health, Education and Welfare, U.S. Government Printing Office, Division of Printing, Washington, D.C., p. 2.

State v. Brown, 112 Minn., 370, 128 N.W., p. 294.

Support Personnel for the Counselor: Their Technical and Non-Technical Roles and Preparation, Personnel and Guidance Journal, April, 1967.

Survey of Public School Teacher Aides, State Education Department, University of the State of New York, Bureau of School and Cultural Research, Albany, The Departmental, April, 1966.

Teacher Aides in the Classroom, A Digest, A New England Study Prepared by the New England Educational Assessment Project, A Cooperative Regional Report of the Six New England States, Providence, Rhode Island, 1967, p. 8.

Teacher Aides in Large School Systems, Educational Research Service Circular, No. 2, 1967, Washington, D. C., The Association, April, 1967, NEA Stock No. 219-06234, p. 1-2.

To What Extent Can Teacher Aides Free The Teacher's Time To Teach? U.S. News and World Report, May 11, 1956.